T0343492

COMPACT

KEY
FOR SCHOOLS
SECOND EDITION

WITH AUDIO
DOWNLOAD

A2

WORKBOOK
WITHOUT ANSWERS

Frances Treloar
For the revised exam from 2020

Cambridge University Press

www.cambridge.org/elt

Cambridge Assessment English

www.cambridgeenglish.org

Information on this title: www.cambridge.org/9781108614047

© Cambridge University Press & Assessment and UCLES 2019

First published 2014
Second edition 2019

20 19

Printed in Great Britain by CPI Group (UK) Ltd, Croydon CR0 4YY

A catalogue record for this publication is available from the British Library

ISBN 978-1-108-61404-7 Workbook without answers with Audio Download

Contents

1	My family, my friends & me	4
2	In my free time	8
3	Eating in, eating out	12
4	What are you doing now?	16
5	Great places to visit	20
6	Getting there	24
7	School rules!	28
8	We had a great time!	32
9	What's on?	36
10	Are you an outdoors person?	40
11	Healthy body, healthy mind	44
12	Technology & me	48
	Vocabulary Extra	52
	Audio scripts	58

1 My family, my friends & me

Grammar

have got

1 Write sentences or questions and short answers with the correct form of *have got*.

1 John and Joe / black hair
   John and Joe have got black hair.

2 Muhammed / blue eyes? / Yes
   Has Muhammed got blue eyes? Yes, he has.

3 We / six cousins
   ....

4 she / older sister? / Yes
   ....

5 I / not / a younger brother
   ....

6 Harry / very short fair hair
   ....

7 your friends / nicknames? / No
   ....

8 They / not / their trainers with them
   ....

2 ⊙ Exam candidates often make mistakes with *have got*. Correct the mistakes in these sentences.

1 I got a free day at the weekend. ..*have got*......
2 I get a new job near home. ....
3 I got flu and am lying in bed now. ....
4 I get a new room. ....
5 I bought strange shoes because everyone got them. ....
6 We've to bring a pencil and a rubber. ....
7 It haven't got a radio. ....
8 I've terrific news. There's going to be a concert in Rillieux. ....

Present simple

3 Read the information about Laura and complete the sentences.

	On school days	In the holidays
wake up	6.50	9.45
walk to school	8.25	–
have lunch	12.20	1.00
do homework	6.30	–
watch TV	7.00	10.00, 2.00, 8.00
go to bed	9.15	10.30

1 Laura ..*wakes up*...... at ten to seven on school days.
2 She .... at twenty-five past eight on school days, but she .... in the holidays.
3 She .... at one o'clock in the holidays.
4 She .... her homework at 6.30 on school days, but she .... any homework in the holidays.
5 She .... TV a lot in the holidays.
6 She .... at quarter past nine on school days.

Question words

4 Complete the questions with the words in the box.

> How   What   ~~What time~~
> When   Where   Who

1 ..*What time*.... do you get up on school days?
2 .... do you travel to school?
3 .... do you have for breakfast?
4 .... is your school?
5 .... is your best friend?
6 .... does your next school holiday start?

5 Answer the questions in Exercise 4 for you. Write complete sentences.

1 ..*I get up at half past seven on school days.*.........

Vocabulary

1 Use the family tree to complete Joanna's sentences with the words in the box.
There are some words you do not need.

> sister   wife   cousins   nephew   daughter   grandmother   children
> niece   husband   ~~sisters~~   Uncle   father   son

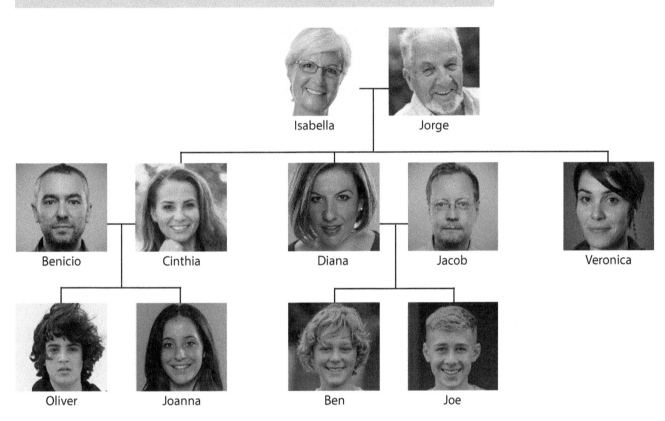

Isabella   Jorge

Benicio   Cinthia   Diana   Jacob   Veronica

Oliver   Joanna   Ben   Joe

1 My name's Joanna. I've got one brother, but I haven't got any *sisters*.

2 I am my parents' only .... My brother, Oliver, is their only ....

3 My Aunt Diana is married to my .... Jacob. Diana is Jacob's ....

4 Diana and Jacob have got two .... – Ben and Joe. Ben and Joe are my ....

5 My aunt Veronica hasn't got a .... – she doesn't want to get married yet.

6 The two people with white hair are my mum's mother and ....

7 My grandfather Jorge is one month younger than my ....

2 🔊 02 Listen and check.

3 Complete the sentences with the phrases in the box.

> do homework   get home   go to bed
> ~~start school~~   wake up   walk to school   watch TV

1 I *start school* at 9.00 every morning.

2 In the morning, I .... at 7.00. Then I get out of bed.

3 I ride my bike to school, but my friend can .... because he lives very near.

4 I leave school on my bike at 3.00 p.m. and .... at 3.15 p.m. My mum is always there.

5 I'm a good student because I .... my .... every day.

6 I like to .... with my family in the evening.

7 At night, I .... early because I need a lot of sleep.

4 🔊 03 Listen and check.

Reading and Writing Part 2

For each question, choose the correct answer.

		Shaziye	Frida	Agata
1	Which person can't visit some of her grandparents?	A	B	C
2	Which person is learning something from one of her grandparents?	A	B	C
3	Which person says one of her grandparents still has a job?	A	B	C
4	Which person lives near all four of her grandparents?	A	B	C
5	Which person lives with one grandparent?	A	B	C
6	Which person finds one thing difficult when she visits her grandparents?	A	B	C
7	Which person eats with her grandmother once a week?	A	B	C

Me and my grandparents

Shaziye

I live with my parents in the city of Bursa, Turkey, and both my mother's and my father's parents live in a village by the sea not far from us. When they were younger, my father's parents lived and worked in Bulgaria. They were both teachers, and came back to Turkey when they finished work. I'm glad we all live in the same country now because we can see each other every week. I love their village, but they always get up very early and I do as well when I stay there. That's not easy for me!

Frida

Six people live in my house in the city of Leon, Mexico. My mother's mother, my parents, my two brothers and me. I'm really lucky because my father's parents also live in a street near our flat, so I visit them nearly every day, too. I call my mother's mother Bela. She had a restaurant and now cooks fantastic meals for us. Mum can't cook well, but I can because Bela's teaching me.

Agata

I often visit my father's parents because they live close to us. But my mother's parents are travelling around the world so it's not possible to go and see them. We often chat on the internet. My father's father works ten hours every week. He's a doctor, so we always phone him when we feel ill. My father's mother was also a doctor, but she doesn't work now. I have lunch with her on Saturdays.

Reading and Writing Part 7

Look at the three pictures.

Write the story shown in the pictures.

Write 35 words or more in your notebook.

Listening Part 3

🔊 04 **For each question, choose the correct answer.**

You will hear Kelly talking to her mum about her singing lessons.

1 When is Kelly's next singing lesson?
   A 8th August
   B 15th August
   C 22nd August

2 Where will they get the music book from?
   A the bookshop
   B the library
   C the music shop

3 Which day will they get the book?
   A Tuesday
   B Wednesday
   C Thursday

4 Kelly's mum will meet Kelly at
   A 3.45 p.m.
   B 4.00 p.m.
   C 4.15 p.m.

5 What kind of food does Kelly want to eat afterwards?
   A pizza
   B fish
   C burgers

2 In my free time

Grammar

Adverbs of frequency

1 Write sentences about Danny's week with the words and phrases in the box.

> every day except Sunday   never   often
> on Sundays   ~~once a week~~   twice a week

Monday	Go to school in Dad's car, piano lesson 5.15 p.m., band practice 6.00 p.m.
Tuesday	Go to school in Dad's car, band practice 6.00 p.m.
Wednesday	Walk to school, swimming club after school, band practice 5.30 p.m.
Thursday	Go to school in Dad's car, band practice 5.00 p.m.
Friday	Walk to school, band practice 4.00 p.m.
Saturday	Swimming club 10.00 a.m., band practice 6.00 p.m.
Sunday	Visit Grandpa as usual!

1 have / a piano lesson
   Danny has a piano lesson once a week.
2 have / band practice ....
3 go / to school in his dad's car ....
4 visit / his grandfather ....
5 have / swimming club ....
6 go / to art club ....

2 ⊘ Exam candidates often make mistakes with words which describe frequency. Correct the mistakes in these sentences.
1 The news media ~~always must~~ have something to put in their headlines.   *must always*
2 We have gone every day to the beach. ....
3 First we eat salad, with sometimes tomatoes, carrots and garlic. ....
4 She likes always to study. ....
5 On holiday I eat it often. ....
6 My son is every day sick. ....
7 I drink juice always. ....

Do you like ...? / Would you like ...?

3 Complete the conversation with the correct form of would like, like or don't like.

Julian: Did you go to music club yesterday?
Peter: No, they played jazz and I (1) *don't like* jazz much.
Julian: What kind of music (2) ....?
Peter: Rock, pop, classical – most kinds, but not jazz!
Julian: I (3) .... to come, too. Can I just come or do I have to ask the teacher first?
Peter: Just come when you want to. (4) .... to come with me next week?
Julian: Yes, please. I (5) .... to join so I can learn to play an instrument.
Peter: (6) .... all kinds of music?
Julian: I (7) .... modern music best, but I (8) .... to learn more about classical music and jazz, too.
Peter: Music club will be perfect for you!

4 🔊 05 Listen and check.

Vocabulary

1 Match the person to the picture.

1 Harry likes watching films.
2 Greg loves sleeping in a tent and eating outside.
3 Natalia likes going to concerts with her friends.

4 Celia likes taking pictures with her camera.
5 Noah enjoys playing the guitar and singing.
6 Jack enjoys reading books before he goes to sleep.

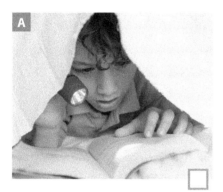

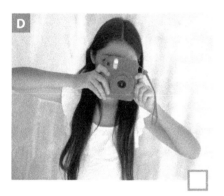

2 Complete the 'opposite' sentences with the words and phrases in the box.

| doesn't like enjoy ~~hates~~ interested in |
| good at prefers terrible at |

1 Ellie loves watching films. Maisie *hates* watching films.
2 Ellie is bad at cooking. Maisie is .... cooking.
3 Ellie enjoys singing. Maisie .... singing.
4 Ellie likes going to concerts. Maisie doesn't .... going to concerts.
5 Ellie is brilliant at playing computer games. Maisie is .... playing computer games.
6 Ellie likes dancing more than doing sports. Maisie .... doing sports to dancing.
7 Ellie thinks history is boring. Maisie is .... history.

3 Complete the sentences for you. Use the correct form of the words and phrases from Exercise 2.

1 I .... cooking.
2 I .... singing.
3 I'm .... at dancing.
4 I'm .... in science.
5 I .... spending time with my family.
6 I .... going to the countryside and learning about nature.

Reading and Writing Part 3

For each question, choose the correct answer.

WHY I LOVE CAMPING

by Helen Menzies

I first went camping when I was ten. I went to France for two weeks with my family and I hated the first week. It was really sunny so our tent was too hot and there were insects in it. But in the second week, I started to like it, and now I love it.

There are lots of good things about camping. We never go to the same place, so there are always new things to see, and it's great to be outside so much. But even better than those things is spending time with my mum, dad and sisters.

When we go camping, I always make new friends. I met Nadia on my first camping trip. I send her an email once a month, but she writes more than me – usually twice a month. I don't have time to write more because I email other friends from camping every week.

We live in a city, so we never camp near cities. My parents love trees and watching nature, so we most often go camping in forests. I like being at the beach, so we sometimes go to the sea, too. Once, we went camping in the mountains, but it was too cold in our tents.

Camping is a great activity for people of all ages. It's never boring because you always have adventures. Once, a horse tried to walk into our tent! Another time, there was a storm and we had to sleep in our car. You never know what will happen.

1 What does Helen say about her first camping holiday?
A She didn't like the type of tent she had.
B She only enjoyed one week of it.
C She felt afraid all the time.

2 What does Helen like most about camping?
A staying in new places
B doing lots of things outside
C being with her family a lot

3 How often does Helen write to Nadia?
A every week
B twice a month
C once a month

4 Where does Helen's family usually go camping?
A in forests
B in the mountains
C by the sea

5 In the last paragraph, Helen says that camping is
A the best activity for people her age.
B a very exciting activity.
C an activity that teaches you a lot.

Listening Part 4

🔊 06 **For each question, choose the correct answer.**

1 You will hear two friends talking about going to art club. What do they say about going to the countryside to paint?
   A They prefer painting inside.
   B They haven't tried painting outside before.
   C They feel happy about painting outside.

2 You will hear a girl talking about a competition. What type of competition was it?
   A a football competition
   B a music competition
   C a tennis competition

3 You will hear a boy talking about joining a dance club. Why does he want to join the club?
   A His friends go to the club.
   B He wants to do something new.
   C It's a good way to exercise.

4 You will hear a girl, Kate, talking to a friend about films. What type of films does she like?
   A comedy films
   B horror films
   C adventure films

5 You will hear two friends talking about a concert they went to. What did they think of the concert?
   A it was too short.
   B it was worse than the last one.
   C it was in a terrible place.

Reading & Writing Part 5

For each question, write the correct answer. Write one word for each gap.

From: Aga

To: Jo

Hi

My name's Agnieszka, but everyone calls **(0)** ....me........ Aga. When I have free time, I enjoy playing all kinds **(1)** .... sport. Table tennis is my favourite game at the moment.

I enjoy table tennis because it's an indoor sport that I can play **(2)** .... it's raining or snowing outside. I get **(3)** .... play it a lot where I live.

Both my sisters love the game too, so I usually play against one of **(4)** .... It really doesn't matter **(5)** .... wins because the most important thing is having fun!

(6) .... do you like doing in your free time? Please write and tell me!

Best wishes,

Aga

3 Eating in, eating out

Grammar

There is / are, a / an, some and any

1 Complete the sentences with *is/isn't/are/aren't* and *a/ an/some/any*.

1 There *is a* chicken in the garden! It's eating the flowers!
2 .... there .... chairs in the kitchen?
3 There .... orange juice in the fridge. Would you like a glass?
4 Why .... there .... egg on the table? Put it back in the fridge, please.
5 There .... clock in the hall, but there's one in the kitchen.
6 There .... rice in the cupboard. We need some more.
7 Do you think there .... vegetables in this soup?
8 There .... exercises in this book that are difficult – they're all easy!

(don't) have to

2 Read the information about the jobs a sister and brother have this week. Complete the sentences with the correct form of *have to* and the appropriate verb.

Job	Emily	Oliver
wash the dishes	✗	✓
tidy the living room	✓	✗
make his/her bed	✓	✓
wash the kitchen floor	✓	✗
tidy his/her bedroom	✓	✓
clean the bathroom	✗	✓

1 Emily *doesn't have to wash* the dishes this week.
2 Oliver *has to wash* the dishes this week.
3 Emily .... the living room this week.
4 Oliver .... the living room this week.
5 Oliver and Emily both .... their beds this week.
6 Emily .... the kitchen floor this week.
7 Oliver .... the kitchen floor this week.
8 Oliver and Emily both .... their bedrooms this week.
9 Emily .... the bathroom this week.
10 Oliver .... the bathroom this week.

3 🔊 **07** Listen and check.

Vocabulary

1 Find the words in the grid below.

chair cupboard cooker desk fridge
lamp mirror shelf shower sofa stairs toilet

S	O	F	A	C	H	A	I	R
F	D	O	C	O	L	F	M	S
C	U	P	B	O	A	R	D	H
S	W	A	E	K	M	I	E	E
T	D	E	A	E	P	D	S	L
A	C	H	M	R	M	G	K	F
I	S	S	H	O	W	E	R	A
R	T	O	I	L	E	T	J	U
S	O	F	M	I	R	R	O	R

2 Write the name of the room next to each description.

1 There's a whiteboard on the wall and there are lots of desks. *classroom*
2 There's a shower and a toilet with a sink next to it. ....
3 There's a TV on the wall, a sofa, a low table and a tall lamp on the floor. ....
4 Between the two beds, there's a cupboard with a clock on it. ....
5 There are lots of cupboards, a fridge and a cooker. ....

3 Match some of the words in the box with the correct picture.

> bread   burger   cheese   chicken   egg
> fish   jam   juice   milk   omelette   onion
> potato (potatoes)   rice   salad   soup

A

B
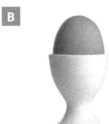

C

D

....

E

F

G

H

....

4 Write the words from the box in Exercise 3 next to the correct sentences.

1 These are two types of type of meat. ....
2 These are two types of vegetables. ....
3 You catch this in the sea. ....
4 This is a drink made with different types of fruit. ....
5 You make this with eggs. ....
6 You make this with fruit and can put it on bread. ....
7 You make dishes like paella and risotto with it. ....
8 You make this from milk. ....
9 You need this to make a sandwich. ....
10 This is a cold dish that often has tomatoes in it. ....

5 Answer the questions for you.

1 What do you eat for breakfast?
   ....
2 Where do you have lunch on school days?
   ....
3 What's your favourite food and drink?
   ....
4 How often do you cook at home?
   ....
5 Do you ever eat in a restaurant? When?
   ....

Reading and Writing Part 4

For each question, choose the correct answer.

THE DAILY LIFE OF A JAPANESE TEENAGER

Akiyoshi is a 13-year-old girl. She lives in Osaka, a Japanese city, with her family.

Every morning, she **(1)** .... breakfast at a low table which is called a 'kotatsu'. After breakfast, she **(2)** .... to school. This only takes five minutes because her school is so **(3)** .... to her house.

She goes to school Monday to Friday and sometimes Saturday mornings, too. Akiyoshi's school subjects **(4)** .... art, music, maths and Japanese. Her class eats lunch in the classroom, then they have to clean the classroom.

When she **(5)** .... home, first, she takes off her shoes. The family's evening **(6)** .... is usually fish or chicken with soup and rice. After eating, she watches TV, does her homework and goes to bed.

1	A comes	B has	C keeps
2	A walks	B brings	C joins
3	A short	B quick	C close
4	A add	B include	C mix
5	A travels	B starts	C returns
6	A meal	B course	C plate

Listening Part 2

🔊 **08** For each question, write the correct answer in the gap. Write one word or a number or a date or a time.

You will hear a woman on TV giving information about a new TV show.

New TV show	
Name:	*Chefs*
First programme about:	(1) ....
Programmes made at:	(2) .... School
Number to call with ideas:	(3) ....
Day:	(4) ....
Start time:	(5) .... p.m.

Reading and Writing Part 7

Look at the three pictures.

Write the story shown in the pictures.

Write 35 words or more.

4 What are you doing now?

Grammar

Present continuous

1 Complete Sarah's and Molly's messages with the present continuous of the verbs in brackets.

> Where are you, Molly?
>
> 11:03 ✓✓

> Hi, Sarah. I **(1)** 'm sitting (sit) on the train to Markham with my mum.
>
> 11:05 ✓✓

> Oh, **(2)** .... (you / go) shopping?
>
> 11:07 ✓✓

> No, we **(3)** .... (not go) shopping. We **(4)** .... (go) to Markham to help my aunt. She **(5)** .... (move) into a new house today. What **(6)** .... (you / do)?
>
> 11:10 ✓✓

> I **(7)** .... (wait) for a bus. I **(8)** .... (go) shopping in Markham!
>
> 11:12 ✓✓

2 Write sentences about the picture with the present continuous of the verbs in brackets. Some sentences need to be negative.

1 (listen) She's listening to music.
2 (eat) ....
3 (drink) ....
4 (wear) ....
5 (sit) ....
6 (hold) ....
7 (run) ....

Present simple vs present continuous

3 Complete the sentences with the correct form of the verbs in brackets.

1 Riley likes (like) skateboarding.
2 I usually .... (practise) with my basketball team on Saturday afternoons.
3 What .... Lucas .... (do) this morning? Can he come with us to the swimming pool?
4 Oscar .... (not want) to go to hockey club again.
5 I can't speak to you at the moment because I .... (play) football.
6 Sophia and Amelia usually .... (play) tennis on Tuesdays.
7 I .... (not do) any sport this week because my leg hurts.
8 On which day .... Leona .... (have) badminton lessons?
9 Dear Harry, how are you? I .... (write) this email to tell you about yesterday's match.

Vocabulary

1 Write *go* or *play* with each word. Then complete the words with *-ing*, *-ball* or *-boarding* to make sports.

1 *go* ski*ing*
2 .... swimm ....
3 .... basket ....
4 .... skate ....
5 .... volley ....

6 .... cycl ....
7 .... ice skat ....
8 .... surf ....
9 .... foot ....

2 Write the names of the sports in Exercise 1 under the correct pictures.

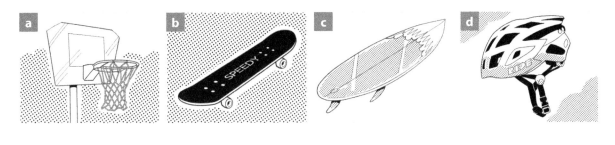

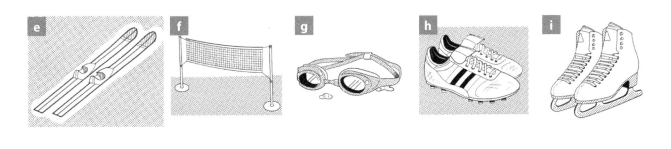

3 Write the letters in the correct order to make sports.

1 s t n i e n .*tennis*...........
2 l o f g ....
3 c e i   c e o k h y ....

4 a l e b t   e s n t n i ....
5 l r a t m a i   r a s t ....
6 s o e r b i c a ....

4 Complete the adjectives with the words in the box.

> warm   fun   pretty   cheap   bright   comfortable

1 A chair that feels nice to sit on is ....
2 Something that you can buy with a little money is ....
3 When it is cold, I wear a sweater because it is ....
4 When you enjoy an activity a lot, it is ....
5 People wear yellow and green jackets for cycling because these colours are ....
6 A dress or skirt that you think looks nice is ....

Listening Part 1

🔊 ⑨ **For each question, choose the correct picture.**

1 Where is Jessie playing table tennis?

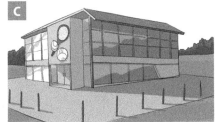

2 What does the girls' football team wear?

3 What time is Henry's skiing lesson?

4 What is the mother's gym teacher doing this evening?

5 Where did Lily put the advertisement for her football ticket?

Reading and Writing Part 1

For each question, choose the correct answer.

1

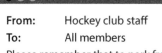

From: Hockey club staff
To: All members
Please remember that to park free at the sports centre, you must leave your member's card in your car window.

What do club members have to do?

A ask staff at the club about where to park
B show their member's card to get free parking
C contact the sports centre about getting a new card

2

LANG RIVER FISHING CLUB
If you catch more than two large fish (over 25 cm) in one day, you must put them back in the river.

A You cannot keep more than two big fish each day.
B You cannot catch more than two big fish each day.
C You can never keep fish that are smaller than 25 cm.

3

Handow Beach
Never surf between red and yellow signs – this area is for swimmers only.

This notice tells people

A why surfing is dangerous at the beach.
B where they cannot go surfing.
C who must not use the beach.

4

From: Freya
To: Alicia
I enjoyed being in the school fashion show. Thanks for lending me your pretty red shoes – they were really comfortable.

A Freya wants some shoes like Alicia's.
B Freya is deciding what shoes to wear for a show.
C Freya borrowed a pair of shoes from Alicia.

5

Summer cycling kit – all half price
HURRY! Last day of sale Friday 23rd August

A Get cycling kit cheaper for one day only in August.
B Cycling kit prices are low until 23rd August.
C On 23rd August, you pay normal prices again for cycling kit.

6

From: Freddie
To: Sam
My brother's driving me to Mandron skateboard park this afternoon. We can pick you up on the way if you want to come.

What is Freddie doing in this message?

A offering Sam a lift later today
B giving Sam advice about activities
C asking Sam for help with transport

Reading and Writing Part 6

Read the email from your English friend, Ali.

Write an email to Ali and answer the questions.

Write 25 words or more.

From: Ali
We've got a new sports centre in our town and I play volleyball there. Where's your nearest sports centre? What can you do there? How often do you go there?

Grammar

Past simple

1 Write the past simple forms.

1 study ....studied....
2 drink ....
3 eat ....
4 enjoy ....
5 try ....
6 start ....
7 find ....
8 open ....
9 go ....

2 Complete the text with the past simple of the verbs in brackets.

3 🔊 ⑩ Listen and check.

4 Write the questions. Then answer them for you.

1 What time / go to bed last night?
What time did you go to bed last night?
I went to bed at half past nine.
2 When / you / born? ....
....
3 What time / get up / this morning? ....
....
4 Where / you / go / last weekend? ....
....
5 What / you / have / for breakfast today? ....
....

Time expressions: *in / at / on; ago*

5 Complete the sentences with *in*, *at*, *on* or *ago*.

1 The shop only opened a month ...., but it's going to close next week.
2 My dad's plane left .... half past six this morning from Heathrow Airport.
3 We enjoyed the concert .... Wednesday – all the bands were brilliant.
4 There wasn't much rain .... December.
5 They arrived in New Zealand .... 16th November.
6 My best friend and I were both born .... 2005.

Last summer, Simon **(1)**went (go) camping with his family near a castle in the mountains in Scotland. It **(2)** .... (be) a beautiful place, but as soon as they arrived, it **(3)** .... (start) to rain and it **(4)** ....(not stop) for days! During the day, they **(5)** .... (not do) any activities because it was too wet outside, and at night, they **(6)** .... (not sleep) because the wind and the rain **(7)** .... (be) so noisy. After four days of rain, the man who lived in the castle **(8)** .... (invite) them to stay with him at the castle! After that, Simon and his family **(9)** .... (have) a great time. They **(10)** .... (not mind) the bad weather because they **(11)** .... (play) games in the castle all day and they **(12)** .... (not hear) the rain and the wind at night.

Vocabulary

1 Match the sentences (1–6) with the words (a–f).

1 People go to this place to see concerts or sports matches.
2 This place is very old and was built to keep the people who lived in it safe.
3 People go to this place to study or to borrow books to read at home.
4 Things like cars, toys and TVs are made in this place.
5 You go to this place to see plays.
6 You go to this place to see things from other centuries and countries.

a a castle
b a factory
c a library
d a museum
e a stadium
f a theatre

2 Match the pictures (1–6) with the places in Exercise 1 (a–f).

3 Complete the sentences with the places in the box.

bank   bookshop   cinema   department store   newsagent   online shop   police station   sports centre   ~~supermarket~~   university

1 I don't like shopping for food in the big *supermarket*. I prefer smaller, local shops.
2 The only thing that the .... in the city centre doesn't sell is food!
3 The .... in my street sells things to read like magazines, but not books.
4 I find studying hard, so I don't want to go to .... after I leave school.
5 Mum went to the .... to ask about borrowing some money.
6 You should phone the .... to ask if anyone has found your laptop.
7 Did you go and see that amazing film at the .... last week?
8 Shall we go to the .... for a game of badminton this afternoon?
9 I often find this .... has cheaper prices than real shops in town.
10 My mum bought a dictionary for me in the .... on Mason Road.

4 Write the dates. Then find out what happened on them.

1 the twenty-second of November, nineteen sixty-three 22/11/1963 *President John F Kennedy died.*
2 the third of August, fourteen ninety-two ....
....
3 the tenth of March, eighteen seventy-six ....
....
4 the fourth of July, seventeen seventy-six ....
....
5 the seventeenth of December, nineteen oh three ....
....
6 the twentieth of July, nineteen sixty-nine ....
....

Reading and Writing Part 2

For each question, choose the correct answer.

		Narith	Toby	Marlon
1	Which person says he learned many things from his visit?	A	B	C
2	Which person would like to buy a Morgan car in the future?	A	B	C
3	Which person visited the factory with someone that does not like cars?	A	B	C
4	Which person had good weather during their visit to the factory?	A	B	C
5	Which person spoke to the people that make the cars?	A	B	C
6	Which person did not have to buy tickets for the tour himself?	A	B	C
7	Which person lives quite near the factory?	A	B	C

My tour of the Morgan car factory

Narith

Last Saturday, I had my first visit to the Morgan car factory. I don't know why I didn't think of going before, because our town is not far from Malvern, where the factory is. I'm so glad my parents gave me and my friend factory tour tickets as a present. What a brilliant two-hour tour! The morning we went was nice and sunny, which was lucky because we had to walk outside a lot. I want to come back in the future and drive one of the cars.

Toby

I love cars, especially old cars, so I was really excited about going to see where Morgans are made. It's quite a long way from my home, and I can't drive, so my cousin Leo gave me a lift and I bought both our tickets. He isn't interested in cars. But even Leo thought the tour was amazing, so you don't have to like cars to enjoy the tour. They use both old and modern ways of working, which taught me a lot about machines and engineering.

Marlon

The tour started with a very good ten-minute information film, and then we walked around the factory. We had a tour with a guide for two hours, but couldn't see some of the outside parts of the factory because there was a thunderstorm. We watched people building the cars, and when I stopped and asked them questions, they didn't mind. I'm going to get a really good job when I'm older, so I can get a Morgan sports car.

Listening Part 2

1 🔊 ⑪ For each question, write the correct answer in the gap. Write one word or a number or a date or a time.

You will hear some information about a museum.

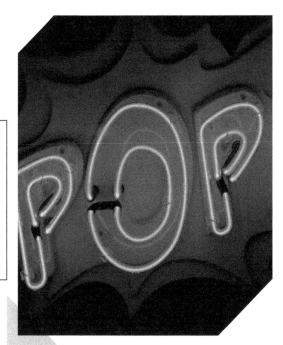

Branton Museum of Pop Music	
Address:	Victoria Square, Branton
Name of this month's exhibition:	**(1)** ....
Date exhibition ends:	**(2)** ....
New room at museum:	**(3)** shows pop stars' ....
Entrance ticket includes:	**(4)** ....
Price for teenagers:	**(5)** £ ....

2 Write questions and answers about the museum in Exercise 1.

1 address?

....

2 name / exhibition?

....

3 when / exhibition end?

....

4 what / in new fashion room?

....

5 entrance ticket includes?

....

6 how much / cost for teenagers?

....

Reading and Writing Part 6

Yesterday you went shopping in a department store.

Write an email to your English friend Sam.

Say:

- **why** you went there
- **how big** the store was
- **what** you liked about the store

Write **25 words** or more.

Write the email in your notebook.

Getting there

Grammar

Comparative and superlative adjectives

1 Complete the sentences with the comparative of the adjectives in brackets.

1 Planes are .... (fast) than buses.
2 Boats are .... (slow) than helicopters.
3 Trains are .... (big) than coaches.
4 Towns are .... (busy) than villages.
5 Motorbikes are .... (expensive) than bicycles.
6 The underground is .... (cheap) than a taxi.

2 ⊙ Exam candidates often make mistakes with superlative adjectives. Correct the mistakes in these sentences.

1 I think the ~~better~~ place you can go is Chalula. ....*best*........
2 I have the best room because it is the most big. ....
3 I love to see the bests football players. ....
4 The Gorillaz is the goodest group that I have ever heard. ....
5 I like the bigest room because I can do anything there. ....
6 It isn't the last technology, but that's not a problem. ....
7 I bought the more beautiful dress that I have ever seen. ....
8 I like best my bedroom. ....

3 Look at the information. Then write sentences using the correct form of the adjectives in brackets.

World train journeys			
	A The Orient Express (Paris to Istanbul)	**B** Pride of Africa (Cape Town to Dar es Salaam)	**C** Deccan Odyssey (Delhi to Mumbai)
Journey time	1 week	2 weeks	8 days
Journey distance	2,256 km	5,743 km	1,161 km
Ticket price (per person)	$11,176	$17,980	$6,100
Date of first journey	1883	1989	2004

Time
1 (short – comparative) Journey A
  is shorter than journey B.
2 (short – superlative) Journey C *is the shortest.*

Distance
3 (far – comparative) Journey A ....
4 (long – superlative) Journey ....

Price
5 (cheap – comparative) Journey A ....
6 (expensive – superlative) Journey ....

Age
7 (old – comparative) Train B ....
8 (new – superlative) Train ....

4 🔊 12 Listen and check.

Vocabulary

1 Look at the key. Then write the correct letters for each form of transport.

> **Key**
> **A** two wheels
> **B** four or more wheels
> **C** usually goes on roads
> **D** flies
> **E** goes on water
> **F** usually carries more than ten people

1 plane   B, D, F
2 lorry   ....
3 bicycle   ....
4 ship   ....
5 car   ....
6 bus   ....
7 train   ....
8 tram   ....
9 motorbike   ....

2 Choose the correct words to complete the sentences.

1 *Bikes / Ships* sail across the sea.
2 A whole class can go on a school trip in a *taxi / coach*.
3 The *plane / underground* is a good way of getting around a city.
4 You can go across the sea and over mountains in a *tram / helicopter*.
5 In very bad weather, riding a *tram / motorbike* is not a good idea.
6 *Lorries / Boats* carry things through the countryside from city to city.

3 Complete the questions with the verbs in the box. Then answer them for you.

> drive   fly   ride   sail   ~~travel~~   walk

1 How do you usually *travel* when you go on holiday?
2 Do most students .... to your school or do they go by bus or car?
3 Which airport do people in your town .... from?
4 Can ten-year-olds .... cars in your country?
5 Does anyone in your family .... a motorbike?
6 How long does it take for a ship to .... around the world?

4 🔊 ⑬ Listen and check. What are the girl's answers? Write the answers in your notebook.

5 Label the signs with the correct words.

> a bridge   a crossing   a roundabout   traffic lights

1 ....

2 ....

3 ....

4 ....

Reading and Writing Part 3

For each question, choose the correct answer.

The lorry driver

My aunt Naomi is a lorry driver. When she left school, she didn't know what she wanted to do, so she went to work in a supermarket. One day, she was talking to one of the lorry drivers at the supermarket, and she decided she wanted to drive a lorry herself. She went home and told her parents (my grandparents!), and they thought it was a good idea.

Naomi's journeys are different every day, and she goes to every part of the country. She enjoys the driving, but she says that one day, she would like to get a job with a different company so she can drive to other countries. Lots of other drivers do this.

Naomi says she likes being out on the road, seeing new towns all the time, but the best thing about driving lorries for her is chatting to everyone she sees during her working day. She also says the lorries are really comfortable, so she doesn't mind sleeping in them. For her, they are her home on wheels!

I asked my grandparents what they thought about Naomi's job. They are happy that Naomi's happy, so they don't want her to change jobs. But they worry about her because it's sometimes a dangerous job and she spends a lot of time away from home.

1   Where did Naomi get the idea to be a lorry driver?
    A at school
    B at work
    C at home

2   What does the second paragraph tell us about Naomi's job?
    A She drives all around the world.
    B She often drives to the same places.
    C She hopes to work for another company in the future.

3   What does Naomi like most about her job?
    A the travelling
    B the people
    C the lorries

4   What do Naomi's parents think about her job?
    A They would like Naomi to do a different job.
    B They are glad it's such an exciting job.
    C They believe the job has some problems.

5   What is the writer doing in the text?
    A explaining how to get one type of work
    B describing someone's work
    C giving advice about doing difficult work

Listening Part 5

🔊 ⑭ For each question, choose the correct answer.

You will hear Marcia talking to her friend Josh about taking the school bus.
Where does each person catch the school bus?

Example:

0 Josh   F

Friends	Places
1 Max ☐	**A** bridge
2 Oliver ☐	**B** car park
3 Emily ☐	**C** cinema
4 Katy ☐	**D** crossing
5 Tom ☐	**E** motorbike shop
	F roundabout
	G traffic lights
	H tram stop

Reading and Writing Part 5

For each number, write the correct answer.

Write one word for each gap.

Example: **0**   *am*

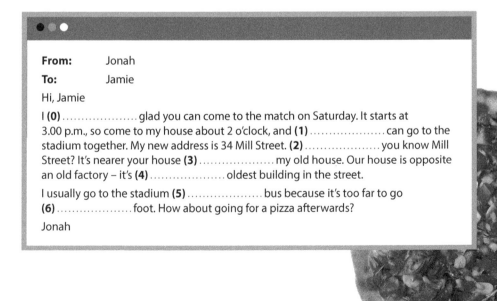

From: Jonah
To: Jamie

Hi, Jamie

I **(0)** .... glad you can come to the match on Saturday. It starts at
3.00 p.m., so come to my house about 2 o'clock, and **(1)** .... can go to the
stadium together. My new address is 34 Mill Street. **(2)** .... you know Mill
Street? It's nearer your house **(3)** .... my old house. Our house is opposite
an old factory – it's **(4)** .... oldest building in the street.

I usually go to the stadium **(5)** .... bus because it's too far to go
(6) .... foot. How about going for a pizza afterwards?

Jonah

7 School rules!

Grammar

must / mustn't

1 Look at the school rules poster. Then complete the sentences with *must/mustn't* and a verb in the box.

> drink   eat   listen   play   ride   show
> take   talk   use   ~~wear~~

In the classroom
1 You *must wear* your school jacket and tie.
2 You .... to music on your phone.
3 You .... water only.
4 You .... pens, pencils and a ruler to your lessons.

In the library
5 You .... your mobile phones.
6 You .... food.
7 You .... to your friends.
8 You .... your library card to the librarian.

In the playground
9 You .... your bike.
10 You .... ball games in the quiet area.

2 Write four things you must and mustn't do in an exam.

> You mustn't copy your friend's answers.
> You must take some pens.

1 ....   2 ....   3 ....   4 ....

should / shouldn't

3 Match Jack's problems (1–6) with the advice (a–f).

1 Jack is always hungry in the afternoon at school.
2 Jack often forgets what his homework is.
3 When it rains, Jack's clothes always get wet.
4 Jack wants to play tennis better.
5 Jack is always tired in the morning.
6 Jack's sister is angry with him.

a He should write it down in a diary or notebook.
b He shouldn't borrow her things without asking.
c He should take an umbrella.
d He should eat more at lunchtime.
e He shouldn't go to bed late.
f He should take some lessons.

4 🔊 15 Listen and check.

5 Complete the sentences. Use your own ideas.

1 Joanna wants to learn to sing. She should *take some lessons* .
2 Paul wants to wake up earlier. He shouldn't ....
3 Georgio wants to learn Spanish. He should ....
4 Deniz wants to read more. She should ....
5 Selina wants to eat better food. She shouldn't ....
6 Ben wants to meet some new people. He should ....

can /could

6 Look at the information.
Then write sentences about Zara.

	Year she began
play badminton	2010
cook vegetable soup	2014
ride a bike	2009
swim	2007
understand 100 English words	2008
play the piano	2009

1 play badminton / 2008
Zara couldn't play badminton in 2008.
2 play badminton / 2011
Zara could play badminton in 2011.
3 play badminton / now
Zara can play badminton now.
4 cook vegetable soup / 2015
....
5 ride a bike / 2010 ....
6 swim / now ....
7 understand 100 English words / 2005 ....
8 play the piano / 2006
....

Adverbs of manner

7 Choose the correct words to complete the sentences.

1 I can't play table tennis very *well / good*.
2 We had to run *quick / quickly* to catch the bus.
3 Harry is *terrible / terribly* at Spanish.
4 Emily and Sophia are learning French very *slow / slowly*.
5 Oliver sang his song *quiet / quietly*.
6 The classroom chairs are not very *comfortable / comfortably*.
7 After the exam, the students walked *happy / happily* out of the classroom.

Vocabulary

1 Write the school subjects.

1 .... 2 .... 3 ....

....

2 Choose the correct words to complete the sentences. Then write sentences for you.

1 Hassan only *has / goes* lessons at school in the morning.
I have lessons in the morning and in the afternoon.
2 Hassan *studies / teaches* 14 different subjects at school.
3 A man called Mr Ali *learns / teaches* Hassan maths.
4 Hassan *spends / uses* about two hours a night doing his homework.
5 Hassan only *learned / missed* one day of school this year.
6 Hassan was very happy when he *passed / studied* his exams last year.

3 🔊 16 Listen and check.

4 Write the letters in the correct order to make instruments. Then match the instruments (1–5) with the pictures (a–e).

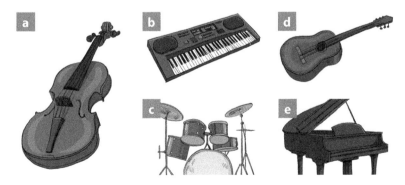

1 r u m s d *drums, c* .....
2 t r a g i u ....
3 i o l v n i ....
4 b k o e y a d r ....
5 n i o p a ....

Reading and Writing Part 1

For each question, choose the correct answer.

1

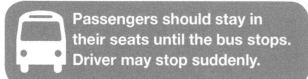

Passengers should stay in their seats until the bus stops. Driver may stop suddenly.

A Passengers should never ask the driver to stop.

B Passengers should not stand up before the bus stops.

C Passengers should stand up when their bus stop is near.

2

MUSIC MAKERS

Please check your change carefully before you leave the shop.

A If customers buy the wrong thing, they can bring it back.

B Customers should look at the money they get back after paying.

C Customers need to be careful while they are in the shop.

3

Want guitar lessons but don't have a guitar?

Two available to borrow – see Mr Titchmarsh

Go and speak to Mr Titchmarsh if you want to

A use a guitar.

B book a guitar teacher.

C learn about different guitars.

4

From: Lars

Hans, I think we'll need to leave for the airport 30 minutes earlier than we agreed – my mum says the traffic's terrible on Fridays.

What is Lars telling Hans?

A His mother will take them to the airport.

B They should use a different type of transport.

C Getting to the airport will take longer than they thought.

5

Students' room

Use the sitting area for chatting, not the study area.

A You must not use the sitting area for studying.

B You must leave the students' room to talk.

C You must be quiet in the study area.

6

To: Class 8
From: Ms Tucker
Subject: Castle trip

You don't need to wear uniform, but there'll be a long walk, so shoes must be comfortable.

Ms Tucker wants the students to

A decide if they want to go walking.

B wear shoes that are good for walking.

C take uniforms to put on after a walk.

Listening Part 2

🔊 ⑰ For each question, write the correct answer in the gap.
Write one word or a number or a date or a time.

You will hear a teacher telling students about some music lessons.

After-school music lessons	
Name of teacher:	Mrs Clarke
Instrument she teaches:	(1) ....
Day of lesson:	(2) ....
Room number:	(3) ....
Name of book to buy:	(4) ....
Price per month:	(5) £ ....

Reading and Writing Part 6

1 👁 Exam candidates often make mistakes in Part 6 emails.

1   What is missing from the email?
2   Correct the underlined mistakes.

Next week I go to an interesting place near your town. I'd really like it there. The place is near the lake and it has a caffe. I like look around it because is very interesting. Usually, here are a lot of people sining and dancing. It's grate. I like here because it's very interesting.

2 Read the email from your English friend, Nicky.

From:	Nicky
To:	

I love singing at school. We sing every morning. What music do you play or listen to at school? What instrument would you like to learn at school? Where do you listen to or play music when you are not at school?

Write an email to Nicky and answer the questions.

Write 25 words or more in your notebook.

8 We had a great time!

Grammar

Past continuous

1 What were the people doing at midnight on New Year's Eve? Write complete sentences.

1 They *were dancing.*
2 He ....
3 They ....
4 They ....
5 They ....
6 She ....
7 I ....

2 Write negative sentences about the people in Exercise 1.

1 They / not sleep *They weren't sleeping.*
2 He / not dance ....
3 They / not study ....
4 They / not sing ....
5 They / not drink coffee ....
6 She / not laugh ....
7 I / not do an exam ....

Past simple and past continuous

3 Complete the sentences with the past simple or past continuous of the verbs in brackets.

1 He .... (not stop) laughing while he .... (watch) the cartoon.
2 The bowl .... (fall) on her foot while she .... (put) fruit in it.
3 They .... (see) the circus lorries in the street while they .... (walk) to school.
4 He .... (break) the light on his bike while he .... (try) to repair the wheel.
5 She .... (play) a computer game, so she .... (not hear) the phone.
6 We .... (build) a fire for the first time while we .... (camp).

4 🔊 **18** Listen and check.

Vocabulary

1 Match what the young people are saying to the place they are staying.

1 Our room's perfect. There's a pool and a nice restaurant here, too.

2 I'm with my mum and brother in a forest. We sleep in a big tent – it's wonderful!

3 We're not going anywhere because I need to study for my exams.

4 The people here are really friendly and I love their house. We all eat together every evening.

a They're staying at a campsite
b They're staying in a hotel.
c They're staying with a family.
d They're staying at home.

2 Complete the sentences with the words in the box.

| try   explore   ~~have~~   learn   speak   visit |

1 It's nice to .*have*............ a rest in a café when you are sightseeing.
2 My parents can .... two other languages well: French and German.
3 In China, I only went to Shanghai - I didn't .... the capital city, Beijing.
4 Before I go to another country, I like to .... the language in a class.
5 When you are in a new place, it's best to .... it on foot – you see so much more.
6 I love to .... new dishes when I go to different parts of my country.

3 Choose the correct words to complete the sentences.

1 We went to some .*brilliant*....... (*brilliant / terrible*) street markets and I bought lots of presents for my family.
2 We visited lots of .... (*funny / interesting*) places, so I learned a lot about the city.
3 When we explored the area around the castle, it was .... (*wonderful / tiring*) because we had to climb a big hill.
4 We didn't enjoy the museum much – we all thought it was .... (*excellent / boring*).
5 We went on a boat trip and saw some whales! It was so .... (*exciting / tiring*).
6 One .... (*funny / terrible*) thing happened when we were standing in the famous square: a bird flew down and sat on my dad's head!
7 We had a really .... (*OK / amazing*) time at the lake. We learned how to sail in one day!

Listening Part 5

For each question, choose the correct answer.

🔊 19 You will hear Matthew talking to Alice about courses their friends took while they were on holiday. Which course did each friend take?

Example:

0 Alice   H

FRIENDS		COURSES
1 Ahmet		**A** cooking
2 Zena		**B** dance
3 Leah		**C** jewellery-making
4 Mick		**D** language
5 Ellie		**E** music
		F science
		G water sports
		H writing

Reading and Writing Part 4

For each question, choose the correct answer.

The Tree Hotel is an unusual hotel in a forest in Sweden. People travel from all around the world to **(1)** .... in this hotel because its seven rooms are at the top of trees. Each room looks very different, but you have to **(2)** .... up to all of them – there are no lifts! The newest one, '7th Room', is the largest, with beds for five people. It's also the **(3)** .... of the seven rooms, as it's 10 metres up in a tree. It even has a **(4)** .... for guests to wash in, too. Another room is **(5)** .... the 'The Mirrorcube' because it has mirrors on all its outside walls. The hotel is near the Lule River, a good place to **(6)** .... fishing.

1	**A** spend	**B** stay	**C** visit
2	**A** climb	**B** build	**C** explore
3	**A** highest	**B** shortest	**C** longest
4	**A** fridge	**B** shower	**C** cupboard
5	**A** called	**B** told	**C** described
6	**A** make	**B** play	**C** go

Reading and Writing Part 7

Look at the three pictures.

Write the story shown in the pictures.

Write 35 words or more.

9 What's on?

Grammar

be going to

1 Match the sentence halves.

1 She's putting her violin in its case because
2 He's studying hard because
3 He's phoning his mum from school because
4 He's finding his seat in the theatre because
5 He's waiting in the street because
6 She's putting her sweater in her bag because
7 He isn't enjoying the football match because

a he isn't going to go home for dinner.
b the play is going to start soon.
c she's going to have a music lesson.
d his team isn't going to win.
e it is going to be cold this evening.
f he's going to do an exam tomorrow.
g a bus is going to come soon.

2 🔊 **20** Listen and check.

3 Write questions with *going to* and the words in brackets.

1 Those children look excited. (see the circus?) *Are they going to see the circus?*
2 You're going to bed early. (get up early tomorrow?) ....
3 She's carrying an umbrella. (it / rain?) ....
4 He's reading a guidebook about Portugal. (go / Portugal?) ....
5 Your team has a big basketball match next Saturday. (do / lots of practice this week?)
6 The train is going more slowly now. (it / stop soon?)
7 You've put the plates, knives and forks on the table. (we / have dinner soon?)

Infinitives and *-ing* forms

4 Complete the sentences with the correct form of the verb in brackets.

1 The guitarist would like ..*to play*........ (play) in a famous band.
2 The photographer hopes .... (take) some good pictures of the mountains today.
3 The actor is very good at .... (show) how he feels.
4 The artist thinks it is difficult .... (find) a good place to have an exhibition of her art.
5 The journalist is interested in .... (write) an article about circus children.
6 The dancer enjoys .... (practise) his dance outside.
7 The drummer doesn't mind .... (sit) behind the other musicians in the band.

Vocabulary

1 Complete the sentences with the correct words.

1 Harry and James are going to the cinema to see a .film...........
2 Dana is going to watch some great actors in a ....at the theatre.
3 Ed and Kyle are going to see a band playing in a ....tomorrow night.
4 George is going to a ....to watch some clowns.
5 Kate is going with her friends to a ....with music from the 1980s.
6 Simon and I are going to look at some paintings at an art ....
7 Mo is having a ....at his house on Saturday to celebrate his birthday.

2 Write the words in the box next to the correct TV programmes.

> a cartoon   a music programme   a quiz show   a sports programme
> the news   the weather

Channel 21		
3.00 p.m.	Two teams of teenagers answer questions about history, art and science. The best team wins a trip to Peru.	1 ....
3.30 p.m.	Funny dinosaur Matty plays amazing games with his new friend Mouse.	2 ....
3.45 p.m.	Ed Sheeran in concert in Liverpool.	3 ....
4.00 p.m.	Learn what's happened today from our journalists around the world.	4 ....
4.15 p.m.	Find out if it's going to rain or stay fine tomorrow.	5 ....
4.20 p.m.	Match between Manchester United and Real Madrid.	6 ....

3 Add -r, -er, -or, -ist or -ian to make words for the people who do these verbs.

1 painter
2 art...................
3 music...................
4 write...................
5 photograph...................
6 guitar...................
7 act...................

4 Write the words. Find out if you don't know the answers.

1 The musician Paco de Lucía was a ....
2 The musician Beyoncé is a ....
3 The musician Lars Ulrich is a ....
4 Pablo Picasso was an ....
5 Scarlett Johannson is an ....
6 Ana Pavlova was a ....

Reading and Writing Part 3

For each question, choose the correct answer.

If you have decided to be a doctor or an engineer, it's easy to get information about how to become one. It's more difficult if you want to be an actor. Nobody can say, 'First you do this, then you do that, and one day you're an actor.' But I can tell you some things that will help.

Learning to be an actor usually starts at school. Drama lessons and clubs can teach students many things, including different ways of acting and how to write their own plays. Writing helps you understand a lot about acting. But even more important is learning to work in a group with other actors.

However, school lessons and clubs are only one part of learning about being an actor. Find small theatre groups near where you live – and don't worry about being the star! It doesn't matter if you only have one word to say in a play, it will still help you improve. You need to be on stage as much as possible, in a variety of different types of plays.

When you finish school, you should think about studying at university. Of course, it's possible to be an actor without going to university, but doing a theatre course is a good idea for some people. These courses may improve your acting, and also help you learn about a variety of subjects, such as business, history, music and dance.

1 What does the writer say is difficult if you want to act?
   A deciding if it's a good job for you
   B finding out what you need to do
   C telling people why you want to do it

2 What does the writer believe is the most useful thing to learn at school?
   A writing for the theatre
   B being part of a team
   C acting in plays

3 What advice does the writer give in the third paragraph?
   A Practise acting outside school.
   B Meet theatre stars who live near you.
   C Learn about all kinds of jobs in theatres.

4 What does the writer think about university for people who want to be actors?
   A It is the best thing to do after school.
   B It is good if they study lots of subjects.
   C It is not always important for them.

5 What is the best title for this text?
   A My life as an actor
   B How to become an actor
   C Different types of acting jobs

Listening Part 4

🔊 **21** **For each question, choose the correct answer.**

1   You will hear a girl talking about a job she wants to do.
    What does she want to be?
    A   an artist
    B   a journalist
    C   a teacher

2   You will hear Ravi talking to his dad.
    What are they discussing?
    A   when a sports programme will finish
    B   when Ravi should do his homework
    C   when is the best time to have dinner

3   You will hear Holly talking about going to the library.
    Why is she going there?
    A   to collect a book
    B   to take a book back
    C   to order a book

4   You will hear Rosie telling her mum about an exhibition.
    What was wrong with the exhibition?
    A   Rosie didn't understand the pictures.
    B   Rosie couldn't see the whole exhibition.
    C   Rosie didn't like the artist.

5   You will hear a boy talking to his mum about his lunch.
    What is he going to make for lunch?
    A   some soup
    B   some sandwiches
    C   some salad

Reading and Writing Part 6

Your friend Paddy has asked you to go to the cinema with him on Wednesday.

Write an email to Paddy.

Say:

• **why** you can't go on Wednesday

• **when** you would like to go

• **which** film you want to see.

Write **25 words** or more.

Grammar

will / won't and may

1 Complete the sentences with *will*, *won't* or *may*.

1 We're staying on an island where it's always sunny, so I .....won't....... take my scarf and gloves.

2 Let's try this path – it .... go to the car park. I hope so, anyway!

3 There's going to be a bad storm this evening, so I've decided I .... go for a run.

4 It .... rain today because it's cloudy, but I'm not sure.

5 I .... wear my warm coat to school today because it's so cold.

6 We .... walk to the top of the hill because we haven't got time.

First conditional

2 Complete the sentences with the correct form of the verbs in brackets.

1 She 'll go (go) to the lake with Nick if he doesn't have (not have) football practice.

2 If she .... (go) to the lake, she .... (need) her swimming costume.

3 If she .... (take) a picnic, she .... (not need) to buy food in the café.

4 If she .... (cycle) around the lake, she .... (feel) tired.

5 If she .... (see) some interesting animals, she .... (take) photos of them.

6 She .... (put) her camera in her bag if it .... (start) to rain.

7 She .... (not take) her umbrella if the weather .... (be) good.

3 🔊 22 Listen and check.

4 👁 Exam candidates often make mistakes with the first conditional. Correct the mistakes in these sentences.

1 I'm the happiest girl in the world if I find it. I'll be

2 I am sure when I go back home I am tired. ....

3 If you like, we would go by car. ....

4 If I can, I am going. ....

5 We will pick you up from the airport when you'll arrive at about 10.30 a.m. on the 20th of June. ....

6 If you need some information about these studies, you would not find it here. You need to look online. ....

Vocabulary

1 Where are these people? Write the places in the box next to the correct sentences.

by a gate	in a field	in a wood	~~on a farm~~	on a
hill	on a lake	on a path	on a river	

1 I'm staying here with my uncle. He's got cows, chickens and two horses. on a farm

2 I'm on a boat tour, travelling through Paris. ....

3 There are lots of sheep eating grass here and a gate in one corner of it. ....

4 It's great walking on this because no cars or bikes can use it – it's not wide enough. ....

5 I couldn't open it, so I had to climb over it. ....

6 Wow! I'm at the top and I can see villages and the countryside below me. ....

7 I'm lost because all the trees here look the same! ....

8 There are trees all around it and we're sailing across it. ....

2 Complete the sentences with *summer*, *spring*, *autumn* or *winter*.

1 In the ...., it is hotter than any other season.

2 The .... is colder than any other season.

3 Leaves are red and brown, and they fall off trees in the ....

4 Plants start to grow again in the ....

5 In Europe, the days are longer and nights are shorter in the ....

6 There is more ice in the .... than in the other seasons.

7 The season before the summer is the ....

8 In Australia, it is the .... when it is the summer in Europe.

3 Write the weather words in the box under the correct pictures.

> cloud   fog   ice   rain   snow   sun
> thunderstorm   wind

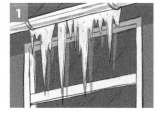

....

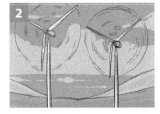

....

....

....

....

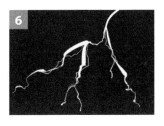

....

....

....

☑ Exam tasks

Reading and Writing Part 7

Look at the three pictures.

Write the story shown in the pictures.

Write 35 words or more.

Listening Part 1

🔊 **23** For each question, choose the correct answer.

1 What was the weather like last winter?

 A
 B
 C

2 Who will go for the birthday meal with Jade and her parents?

 A
 B
 C

3 What happened during the storm last week?

 A
 B
 C

4 What does Eleanor do on the farm at weekends?

 A
 B
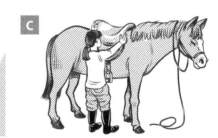 C

5 Where is Charlie's phone?

 A
 B
 C

Reading and Writing Part 1

For each question, choose the correct answer.

1

Knight's Park West Gate
Exit only.
To enter park, use North Gate.

A The West Gate is closed at the moment.
B The West Gate is the only entrance to the park.
C The West Gate is where you go out of the park.

2

```
●  ● ●
```
To: Windsurfing Course students
From: Hannah (teacher)
Please call me each morning to find out if the weather's good enough for lessons to take place.

A Students will learn to check the weather during their windsurfing lessons.
B Students should get information from the teacher before every windsurfing lesson.
C Today's lesson is not happening because the teacher cannot get there.

3

This week's special offer:
get a free T-shirt with
clothes orders
over £20!

What is this week's special offer?

A The clothes you can buy here are cheaper than usual.
B If you spend more than £20 on clothes, you get a gift.
C All the clothes except T-shirts cost just £20.

4

 Children are welcome at the factory's visitor centre, but they must be with an adult at all times and they must be 13 or over to join factory tours.

If you are 12 years old or younger, you cannot

A visit the factory with an adult.
B enter the visitor centre.
C go on a tour of the factory.

5

Our company offers special coach travel to concerts, from towns across the country to the gates of the Meadow Stadium.

This is an advertisement for

A transport.
B concert tickets.
C stadium tours.

6

Bus timetable R-67

This gives details for Monday to Saturday only. Download timetable R-68 for Sundays.

A Bus times are different from timetable R-67 on three days of the week.
B You should check online every day for changes to bus times.
C If you want to travel on a Sunday, you will need another timetable.

11 Healthy body, healthy mind

Grammar

Present perfect; *just / yet / already*

1 Complete the questions with the correct form of the verbs in brackets. Then write short answers that are true for you.

Have you ever ...

1 bought (buy) a newspaper?
  No, I haven't. / Yes, I have.

2 .... (fly) in a helicopter?
  ....

3 .... (take) a photo of a pet?
  ....

4 .... (catch) a fish?
  ....

5 .... (forgot) to brush your teeth?
  ....

6 .... (see) a white rabbit?
  ....

7 .... (be) in a school play?
  ....

8 .... (do) your homework on a bus?
  ....

9 .... (hear) yourself speaking on a recording?
  ....

10 .... (eat) an insect?
  ....

2 Complete the conversation with *just*, *yet* or *already*.

Dad: Hi, Adam. What are you doing? Have you had dinner (1) yet?
Adam: No, I've (2) .... got home from my music lesson.
Dad: Oh, are you hungry?
Adam: Yes, I am. Do you want me to help you cook?
Dad: No, I've (3) .... done it. I made some fish soup earlier this evening, so it's all ready.
Adam: Great! Let's eat. I'll lay the table.
Dad: I've (4) .... done that too. But I haven't put any water or glasses on the table (5) .... Can you do that, please?
Adam: OK.

3 🔊 24 Listen and check.

4 Complete the sentences with the correct form of the verbs in the box.

drink	eat	not finish	not have	read
run	sit	~~start~~	win	

1 It has just started to rain, so I'm going inside.
2 Maggie is a very good singer – she .... already .... three competitions this year.
3 They .... lunch yet because they're still cooking it.
4 I won't borrow that book because I .... already .... it.
5 Stand up quickly! You .... just .... on my glasses!
6 He .... his homework yet because his friend phoned while he was doing it.
7 She .... just .... a whole bottle of water because the race made her very thirsty.
8 You can't have another biscuit because we .... already .... all of them!
9 I need a glass of water because I .... just .... all the way home from school.

Present perfect with *for* and *since*

5 Write two sentences for each prompt using *for* and *since*.

1 I / not see Frankie / two months / April
  I haven't seen Frankie for two months.
  I haven't seen Frankie since April.

2 He / be / a waiter / 2016 / three years
  ....
  ....

3 The cat / not eat anything / Tuesday / two days
  ....
  ....

4 We / live in this house / 10 years / 2009
  ....
  ....

5 I / have this bike / I was 12 years old / five years
  ....
  ....

6 She / be in the shop / an hour / three o'clock
  ....
  ....

7 They / not speak to each other / last Sunday / six days
  ....
  ....

Vocabulary

1 Write the letters in brackets in the correct order to complete the sentences.

1 Cats have four (e s g l) _legs_.
2 At the dentist's, you have to open your (o t h m u) ....
3 We have fingers on our (n a d h s) ....
4 A baby's first (o t o t h) usually grows when it is about six months old. ....
5 Horses don't have any (s a m r) ....
6 Some men have a beard on their (a c e f) ....
7 When you sleep, you close your (y e e s) ....
8 If you eat too much, you will get a big (a c s o t m h) ....
9 Old people often have grey or white (r h i a) ....
10 You sit on a horse's (a k c b) ....
11 You put a shoe on your (o f o t) ....
12 We have a (o n s e) .... in the middle of our face.
13 You listen with your (r e s a) ....
14 Your (e c n k) is between your head and your body.

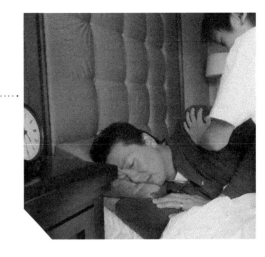

2 Match the sentence halves.

What's the matter?

1 I burnt my mouth because I
2 I went to the dentist because I
3 I put a plaster on my finger because I
4 Don't talk loudly please because I
5 I feel very hot because I
6 I'm not hungry because I
7 I can't walk because I
8 I can't write because I

a have got a headache.
b have got a temperature.
c drank some hot tea.
d had toothache.
e have got a stomach ache.
f cut it.
g have hurt my hand.
h have got a broken leg.

3 Put the words into the correct category.

afraid   angry   bored   glad   great   happy   sick   sorry   unhappy

+ feelings ☺	– feelings ☹
	afraid

4 Write the words in the box under the correct pictures.

afraid   angry   bored   happy   sick   tired

  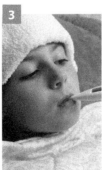    

1 _happy_ 2 .... 3 .... 4 .... 5 .... 6 ....

Reading and Writing Part 4

For each question, choose the correct answer.

MEDICINE FOR MY HEADACHE

I have just returned from a holiday in the mountains of Peru. I (1) .... walking with my family. My parents have (2) .... me on other holidays in mountain areas, but the mountains in Peru are the highest I've (3) .... seen.

One day, we walked through a beautiful old village. I had a headache because we were so high up in the mountains. I started to talk to a woman who lived there, and told her about my headache. She went to a plant that was (4) .... near us, picked a few flowers from it and made some tea with them in her kitchen. She gave me the tea and it made me feel (5) .... Soon, my head stopped (6) .... I was so glad I talked to that woman!

1	**A** did	**B** went	**C** got
2	**A** gone	**B** put	**C** taken
3	**A** ever	**B** never	**C** before
4	**A** standing	**B** growing	**C** looking
5	**A** better	**B** best	**C** favourite
6	**A** hitting	**B** hiding	**C** hurting

Listening Part 3

🔊 25 For each question, choose the correct answer.

You will hear Christina talking to her friend Leo about a health problem.

1 When is Christina going to see the doctor?
A today
B tomorrow
C on Thursday

2 Christina hurt herself when she was
A going up some stairs.
B practising basketball.
C walking to school.

3 Where is Christina now?
A in her bedroom
B in the living room
C in the kitchen

4 Christina is unhappy because she cannot
A play her guitar.
B skateboard.
C go swimming.

5 Christina is going to read Leo's book about
A a film star.
B a pop star.
C a sports star.

Reading and Writing Part 2

For each question, choose the correct answer.

		Kemal	Dan	Jerzy
1	Which person has decided something about his future because of the project?	A	B	C
2	Which person had to find out about some things that make us sick?	A	B	C
3	Which person was unhappy about explaining his project to his classmates?	A	B	C
4	Which person did a project which only included work that was written?	A	B	C
5	Which person thinks he can actually use what he learned?	A	B	C
6	Which person planned something to put on the internet?	A	B	C
7	Which person had to describe how some parts of the body work?	A	B	C

My project about health and the body

Three students write about a project they have done.

Kemal

For my project, I had to find out about our teeth, mouth and stomach. I had to find pictures of them and explain what happens to food, from the moment we put it in our mouths to when it goes into our stomachs. Then I gave a talk about it all to my class. Writing the project was interesting and I learned a lot about the body, but I didn't like giving the talk – I felt really worried before I did that.

Dan

I did a project about why and how we get some health problems, such as colds, having a temperature, toothache and pain. With all the information I found, I had to make a web page for teenagers to use. I enjoyed doing the project, especially the talk to my class at the end. After the talk, I gave them a quiz and they answered everything really well. Perhaps I should be a teacher in the future!

Jerzy

My project was about what you should do when people get ill suddenly or hurt themselves, so it was really useful. For example, I now know how to help a friend who has cut himself badly, or a family member who has broken an arm or a leg. I had to write a ten-page document for teenagers. I found most of the information I needed online. One thing the project taught me is that I certainly don't want to be a doctor or a nurse when I'm older!

Grammar

The passive: present and past

1 Complete the information with the present passive of the verbs in brackets.

FACTFILE

You Tube **Amazing information about YouTube**

1 Every day, five billion* videos are watched (watch) on YouTube.
2 300 hours of video .... (put) on YouTube every minute.
3 Each month, YouTube .... (visit) 1.57 billion times.
4 YouTube .... (use) in 88 different countries and in 76 different languages.
5 About 20 percent of YouTube videos .... (start) but then left after ten seconds.
6 YouTube videos .... (see) on mobile phones over one billion times a day.
7 Over 3.25 billion hours .... (spent) watching videos on YouTube each month.
* 1 billion = 1,000,000,000

2 Write past passive sentences with **on**, **in**, **of** or **by**.

1 The first email / send / 1971
  The first email was sent in 1971.
2 The first digital cameras / sell / a company called Logitech
  ....
3 The first fridge / build / Jacob Perkins / 1834
  ....
4 The first computer mouse / make / wood
  ....
5 The first hairdryer / use / a French hairdresser
  ....
6 The first text messages / write / 3rd December, 1992
  ....

3 🔊 **26** Listen and check.

4 Complete the sentences with the correct form of the verb in bold.

eat

1 a Last night, the boys *ate* some fish for dinner.
  b The beans I was growing in the garden *were eaten* by birds.

give

2 a Our dog's lucky – it .... a large bowl of food every evening.
  b He's a waiter, so he .... people their food every day at work.

take

3 a Yesterday, Sophie .... to her friend's 12th birthday party by car.
  b Yesterday, Mum .... me and my sisters to the zoo.

ask

4 a Jason's mum always .... him to help when she's doing the washing-up.
  b Jenny .... to tidy her bedroom when her grandmother comes to stay.

as + adjective + (not) as

5 Write the words in the correct order to make sentences.

1 the / as / hot / winter / summer. / not / The / as / is
  The winter is not as hot as the summer.
2 as / physics. / is / interesting / biology / I think / as
  ....
3 are / big / screens. / Mobile phone / as / screens / as / tablet / not
  ....
4 are / as / Lessons at school / as / school trips. / much fun / not
  ....
5 expensive / as / motorbike / my mum's / car! / My dad's / as / was
  ....
6 not / bike / was / as / My / fast / my / new bike. / as / old
  ....

Vocabulary

1 Write the words under the pictures.

....

....

....

....

....

....

....

....

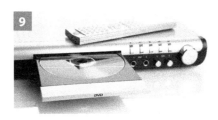

....

2 Complete the sentences with the verbs in the box.

call   chat   download   email address   ~~play~~   text   use

1 I play a football game online with my friends a lot.
2 I'll send it to you. Is your .... kharris@jhmail.com?
3 I often .... music from an online store.
4 I've got your mobile number, so I'll .... you when I arrive – it's cheaper than phoning.
5 I .... the internet a lot for my homework.
6 I need to .... my mum to speak to her about giving us a lift this evening.
7 My friends and I use a few different apps to .... to each other.

3 Match the sentence halves.

1 A lamp is used
2 A case is used
3 A fridge is used
4 A keyboard is used
5 A clock is used
6 A cooker is used
7 A washing machine is used

a to clean your clothes.
b to carry things in and to protect them.
c to tell you the time.
d to make food hot.
e to help you read at night.
f to keep food cold.
g to write on a computer.

Listening Part 5

🔊 **27** For each question, choose the correct answer.

You will hear Alice talking to her mum about the things people in her family want to find on the internet. What does each person want to find?

Example:

0   Dad   C

People		**Things**	
1	Brother	**A**	camera
2	Sister	**B**	clock
3	Cousin	**C**	film
4	Aunt	**D**	holiday
5	Grandmother	**E**	musical instrument
		F	printer
		G	tablet
		H	TV

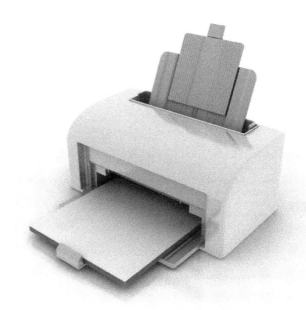

Reading and Writing Part 5

For each question, write the correct answer.

Write one word for each gap.

Example: 0 *or*

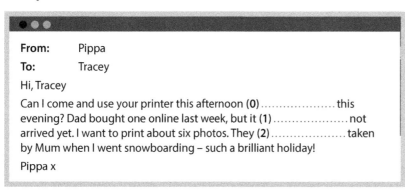

From: Pippa
To: Tracey

Hi, Tracey

Can I come and use your printer this afternoon **(0)** .... this evening? Dad bought one online last week, but it **(1)** .... not arrived yet. I want to print about six photos. They **(2)** .... taken by Mum when I went snowboarding – such a brilliant holiday!

Pippa x

From: Tracey
To: Pippa

Hi, Pippa

Of course you can use my printer. It's **(3)** .... bit slow, but it prints good pictures. **(4)** .... don't you come at 6.00 this evening? You can have dinner **(5)** .... me and my family before we print the photos. When **(6)** .... your dad think your printer will arrive?

Tracey x

Reading and Writing Part 2

For each question, choose the correct answer.

	Charlotte	Abigail	Françoise
1 Which person has already received a prize in a competition?	A	B	C
2 Which person is good at several subjects at school?	A	B	C
3 Which person wants to get a job with a computer games company?	A	B	C
4 Which person was given advice about the competition by someone at school?	A	B	C
5 Which person has made films during school time?	A	B	C
6 Which person was paid to check new computer games when she was younger?	A	B	C
7 Which person made a game for a member of her family?	A	B	C

The computer game competition

Three students write about making a computer game for a competition.

Charlotte

I learned to make games at school in IT and art lessons when I was ten. We made video cartoons. I also worked on the game for this competition at school. Last year, my brother and I made a different game for a school competition, and we won a trip to a computer games company with one of the teachers. When I leave school, I'd love to work there, but I don't think I'll earn a lot.

Abigail

I made the game for fun for my brother. I planned to make a different one for the games competition. However, when I showed it to my IT teacher at school, he thought it was brilliant and said I should enter it! Everyone just loves playing it. I'm really excited about the competition, but I don't think I'm going to win. In the future, I want to start my own technology company.

Françoise

When I was 11, I played video games all the time. So I began to check new video games for a computer games company. We had to play them and find any problems and I earned money for doing it. I also started to get ideas and I began to make the game I'm entering for the competition. I've always worked hard and I usually pass all my art, IT, business and maths exams at school easily. I hope to do a course in computer art at college next year.

Vocabulary Extra

 1 My family, my friends & me

1 Look at the pictures. Match the sentence halves.

1 Everyone in my family has got
2 My cousins Ben and Joe have got
3 I've got
4 My grandmother has got
5 My son is
6 My mother is

a curly hair.
b dark eyes.
c quite tall.
d short dark hair.
e long fair hair.
f short.

2 Choose the word which does not fit.

1	eye	(beach)	hair	face
2	slim	short	tall	thirsty
3	tired	curly	long	straight
4	bedroom	fruit	pizza	burger
5	favourite	best	nice	terrible
6	dark	yellow	brown	fair
7	to	between	in	park
8	glasses	earrings	surname	hat

 2 In my free time

1 Match the phrase halves. Then write the correct numbers in the boxes.

 A
 B
 C
 D
 E
 F

1 play an
2 draw
3 cook a
4 take
5 enter a
6 meet up
7 play
8 play computer
9 go to
10 watch
11 collect
12 dance

a posters
b films
c competition
d with friends
e sports
f photos
g to music
h meal
i pictures
j instrument
k games
l a concert

3 Eating in, eating out

1 Label the photos with words from the box.

balcony   chimney   door   lamp   plants   plant pot   roof   steps   wall   window

1	6 ....
2	7 ....
3	8 ....
4	9 ....
5	10 ....

4 What are you doing now?

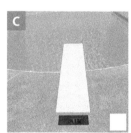

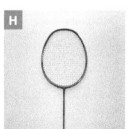

1 Match the words. Then number the pictures.

1	football	a	board
2	badminton	b	racket
3	ice	c	gloves
4	boxing	d	stick
5	hockey	e	net
6	swimming	f	skates
7	basketball	g	boots
8	diving	h	goggles

5 Great places to visit

1 Match the sentence halves.

1	At a bank, you can	**a**	buy some stamps and send a present.
2	At a stadium, you can	**b**	buy a dictionary.
3	In a bookshop, you can	**c**	see a play.
4	In a post office, you can	**d**	buy many different kinds of food.
5	At the theatre, you can	**e**	watch a sports match.
6	In a school canteen, you can	**f**	buy a newspaper.
7	In a library, you can	**g**	study or find a book to borrow.
8	At a police station, you can	**h**	sit and eat your lunch.
9	At a supermarket, you can	**i**	get some money.
10	At a newsagent, you can	**j**	ask for help when you lose something.

2 Write the dates.

1 the twenty-first of October, seventeen eighty-two   21/10/1782
2 the fifth of June, nineteen forty-four
3 the ninth of November, fourteen thirty-two
4 the twelfth of February, sixteen seventy-three
5 the fifteenth of March, eighteen oh three
6 the twenty-third of May, nineteen twelve

6 Getting there

1 Match the pictures with the words in the box.

a bridge   a car park   a corner   a crossing   a road   a roundabout
a motorway   a square   a tunnel   traffic lights

1 ....
2 ....
3 ....
4 ....

5 ....
6 ....
7 ....
8 ....

9 ....
10 ....

7 School rules!

1 Match two activities with each subject.

studying mountains and rivers	art	learning how to find the size of a circle
studying how plants grow	history	drawing
adding numbers	music	reading about things that happened hundreds of years ago
painting	science	learning about weather in different countries
learning grammar	English	singing
learning about past kings and queens	geography	finding out about space
playing an instrument	maths	doing a listening test

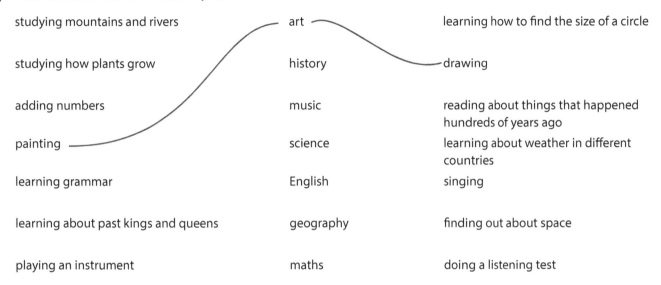

8 We had a great time!

1 Look at the photo. Then complete the questions and answers with the words in the box.

> climbing having speaking staying
> trying visiting

1 What is he doing?
He's ....

2 What kind of places does he like ....?
Places with lots of mountains.

3 Where is he ....?
At a campsite near the mountain.

4 Why isn't he going up the mountain at the moment?
He's .... a rest.

5 What languages is he good at ....?
German and Italian.

6 What is he doing tomorrow?
He's .... a new adventure sport.

2 Write the letters in brackets in the correct order to make adjectives to complete the sentences.

1 I didn't enjoy that book. It was too long and (o r g n i b) *boring*.

2 We had a really (u l w f a) .... time at the lake. It was windy and we couldn't sail.

3 The long journey home was really (d l u l) .... There was nothing interesting to see.

4 That restaurant was (r e t r b e i l) .... – I couldn't eat the meat and the chips were cold.

5 The science museum is really (r t e g a) .... You can learn a lot of new things there.

6 The hotel was (a t l r i i n l b) .... It had three swimming pools, a cinema and shops.

 **What's on?**

1 Where did the people go? There is one word you won't need.

> a circus   a concert   an exhibition   a festival
> a film   a party   a play

1 There were about 50 pictures, all painted by children...................

2 It was at Robert's house, and all my friends were there. It was good fun...................

3 Everyone in the band played so well, and the singing was brilliant...................

4 I didn't think the clowns were very funny...................

5 I loved it, and all the actors are amazing. But we sat very close to the screen, so my neck hurts now!...................

6 We sat at the front of the theatre, so we were very near the actors...................

2 Are the sentences true (T) or false (F)?

1 Cartoons are usually very sad...................
2 You watch the weather to find out if it's going to rain...................
3 The news usually makes you laugh a lot. ....
4 People sometimes win lots of money in quiz shows. ....
5 Music programmes are usually for people aged 70 and over...................
6 Only people who are good at sports watch sports programmes...................

 Are you an outdoors person?

1 In which photo can you see these things? Write A, B or A/B.

1 the sea ....
2 some mountains ....
3 the sky ....
4 some rocks ....
5 wildlife ....
6 a rainforest ....
7 a beach ....
8 some ruins ....
9 a valley ....

2 Match the adjectives with the correct noun.

> clear   rainy   cool   fine   icy

1 A .... day is wet.
2 A .... day is a little bit cold.
3 .... weather is sunny and bright.
4 A .... sky does not have any clouds or fog in it.
5 An .... day is very cold.

11 Healthy body, healthy mind

1 Are the sentences true (T) or false (F)? Correct the false sentences.

1 You see with your ears. ....
2 Your face shows if you are happy or not. ....
3 You put shoes on your feet. ....
4 A dentist helps you look after your teeth. ....
5 People have two noses. ....
6 Eyes can be blue, green or brown. ....
7 Your neck is at the end of your legs. ....
8 You put food in your mouth to eat it. ....
9 You wear a hat on your stomach. ....
10 People have three legs. ....
11 You can hold things in your hands. ....
12 You wear necklaces on your arms. ....

2 Complete the sentences with the words in the box.

| accident ambulance appointment |
| medicine nurse |

1 If you don't feel well, you make an ....
with the doctor.
2 My mum works in a hospital. She's a ....
3 I hurt myself when I had an .... on my bike.
4 You should take some .... if you have a headache.
5 If you are very poorly, you might go to hospital in an ....

12 Technology & me

1 Tick (✓) the correct verbs to complete the phrases. You can tick more than one box for each phrase.

open	visit	reply to	search for	upload	click on	
			✓			a file
						a web page
						a video
						a message
						an email
						information

2 Choose the correct adjective.

1 I called Ben but didn't speak to him because his number was *full / busy*.
2 My new tablet is much *higher / quicker* than my old one. All my apps open immediately.
3 I've got a new phone but it's not the *latest / youngest* model because that was too expensive.
4 My phone screen is *fine / broken* because it fell out of my pocket.
5 Oh no! I can't get on the internet because my phone battery is *sick / dead*.

Audio script

🔊 **02** **Unit 1, Vocabulary, Exercise 2**

1
Joanna: My name's Joanna. I've got one brother, but I haven't got any sisters.

2
Joanna: I am my parents' only daughter. My brother, Oliver, is their only son.

3
Joanna: My Aunt Diana is married to my Uncle Jacob. Diana is Jacob's wife.

4
Joanna: Diana and Jacob have got two children – Ben and Joe. Ben and Joe are my cousins.

5
Joanna: My aunt Veronica hasn't got a husband – she doesn't want to get married yet.

6
Joanna: The two people with white hair are my mum's mother and father.

7
Joanna: My grandfather Jorge is one month younger than my grandmother.

🔊 **03** **Unit 1, Vocabulary, Exercise 4**

1
Girl: I start school at 9.00 every morning.
2
Girl: In the morning, I wake up at 7.00. Then I get out of bed.
3
Girl: I ride my bike to school, but my friend can walk to school because he lives very near.
4
Girl: I leave school on my bike at 3.00 p.m. and get home at 3.15 p.m. My mum is always there.
5
Girl: I'm a good student because I do my homework every day.
6
Girl: I like to watch TV with my family in the evening.
7
Girl: At night, I go to bed early because I need a lot of sleep.

🔊 **04** **Unit 1, Listening Part 3**

Mum: Kelly, I spoke to your singing teacher last night. You haven't got a lesson this week.
Kelly: OK, so when's my next lesson?
Mum: It'll be on the 15th of August– you're missing this week, which is the 8th of August, and on the 22nd of August, your teacher's away again.
Kelly: Right.
Mum: She said you need a new music book, too.
Kelly: Oh, OK. Where can we get that?
Mum: Well, they haven't got any music at the library, I've looked before. The bookshop's cheaper than the music shop, so we'll get it there.
Kelly: OK.
Mum: Which day shall we go?
Kelly: How about Thursday? You work late on Tuesdays and I've got dance club on Wednesday.
Mum: Fine.

Kelly: Will you pick me up after school?
Mum: No, I only finish work at quarter to four, so go home first. I'll see you there at four o'clock. Then we'll get to the shop about quarter past four.
Kelly: Right.
Mum: Would you like dinner in a restaurant afterwards?
Kelly: Yeah! I heard the burger restaurant's closed, but I'd like to go and have a pizza. The fish restaurant's a bit too far from the shops.
Mum: Great!

🔊 **05** **Unit 2, Grammar, Exercise 4**

Julian: Did you go to music club yesterday?
Peter: No, they played jazz and I don't like jazz much.
Julian: What kind of music do you like?
Peter: Rock, pop, classical – most kinds, but not jazz!
Julian: I'd like to come, too. Can I just come or do I have to ask the teacher first?
Peter: Just come when you want to. Would you like to come with me next week?
Julian: Yes, please. I'd like to join so I can learn to play an instrument.
Peter: Do you like all kinds of music?
Julian: I like modern music best, but I'd like to learn more about classical music and jazz, too.
Peter: Music club will be perfect for you!

🔊 **06** **Unit 2, Listening Part 4**

1 *You will hear two friends talking about going to art club. What do they say about going to the countryside to paint?*
Boy: It's Art Club today. Are you coming?
Girl: Yes – we're going outside to paint. I'm glad we are – it's fun doing that.
Boy: Absolutely. I really enjoyed it when we went to the city centre and painted outdoors in the town square.
Girl: Me too. And it will be interesting to paint the fields and the lake.
Boy: Yes, it will.

2 *You will hear a girl talking about a competition. What type of competition was it?*
Girl: I enjoyed the competition. I didn't win, but I played well and I didn't get too tired. But I missed a lot of balls. I wish I'd practised more – I need to hit the ball harder. A lot of the people I played were better than me, but they were older, too. I'll win more games when I'm older.

3 *You will hear a boy talking about joining a dance club. Why does he want to join the club?*
Boy: I'm joining the dance club this month. I always do loads of exercise, like playing basketball and swimming, but I'd like to do an activity I've never done before. At the club, they do dances from around the world, so I'll learn about all kinds of music too. I asked my friends to come along, but they're not interested.

4 *You will hear a girl, Kate, talking to a friend about films. What type of films does she like?*
Boy: What kind of films do you like, Kate?

Girl: Er… I like a few types… though not adventure films. They're a bit boring. Comedy films are too, I think, because nothing exciting happens. And often, they're not even amusing. But you're never bored when you watch a horror film. They're great.

5 *You will hear two friends talking about a concert they went to. What did they think of the concert?*

Girl: Well, what did you think of the concert?

Boy: Not bad! Definitely better than the last concert we went to in that theatre.

Girl: Yes, that's true. That was awful. But it's always nice to go there – the sound quality is amazing. But they didn't play many songs, did they?

Boy: No. They only played for about an hour and a half which wasn't enough.

🔊 07 Unit 3, Grammar, Exercise 3

1
Man: Emily doesn't have to wash the dishes this week.
2
Man: Oliver has to wash the dishes this week.
3
Man: Emily has to tidy the living room this week.
4
Man: Oliver doesn't have to tidy the living room this week.
5
Man: Oliver and Emily both have to make their beds this week.
6
Man: Emily has to wash the kitchen floor this week.
7
Man: Oliver doesn't have to wash the kitchen floor this week.
8
Man: Oliver and Emily both have to tidy their bedrooms this week.
9
Man: Emily doesn't have to clean the bathroom this week.
10
Man: Oliver has to clean the bathroom this week.

🔊 08 Unit 3, Listening Part 2

Man: Now, here's something interesting for all of you teenagers who are interested in TV programmes about food. A new show called *Chefs* is coming to your screens soon. It will include cooking and information about all kinds of subjects, such as healthy food and national dishes.
In the first programme, young cooks tell us all about vegetables. They'll show us how to grow and cook them. But this won't be like a normal TV show: the programmes are not filmed in the TV centre. We're making the programmes at a school! It's called Whiteside School, that's spelt W-H-I-T-E-S-I-D-E. And we'd like you to call us with your ideas – we'll choose the best ones and then you can come and film with us! So phone us on 0996 548013. Now check your diary! This amazing new programme will be on Mondays. And on Tuesday evenings, you'll be able to chat to people from the show online. The first show's on 28th November, from five fifteen until five forty-five – write it down now!

🔊 09 Unit 4, Listening Part 1

1 *Where is Jessie playing table tennis?*
Girl: Where's Jessie, Robert? At the sports centre?
Boy: Well, she's playing table tennis with her friend, Kate, but not at the centre. They went to Kate's place after school.
Girl: To Kate's house, you mean?
Boy: That's right, and they're going to the sports centre to play volleyball after that.

2 *What does the girls' football team wear?*
Boy: Does your team wear black shirts, like ours?
Girl: With white numbers, yes. Our team wears nearly the same as yours, but our socks are white, not black.
Boy: Oh. So you wear white shorts, too?
Girl: We do, with a black number at the sides.
Boy: That sounds great!

3 *What time is Henry's skiing lesson?*
Man: Is your skiing lesson before or after mine this morning, Henry?
Boy: What time's yours, Dad? I can't remember.
Man: It's at 8.45.
Boy: Oh, well, mine starts half an hour later, at quarter past nine. You'll have to get up before me!

4 *What is the mother's gym teacher doing this evening?*
Boy: Why aren't you at your gym class this evening, Mum?
Woman: Our teacher can't do the class this week.
Boy: Is she ill again?
Woman: No, she's fine now. She's flying to Paris tonight because she's going to visit a friend there tomorrow.
Boy: She's lucky – I love flying!

5 *Where did Lily put the advertisement for her football ticket?*
Boy: Lily, hi. Did you sell that football match ticket that you don't want? I just heard someone on the radio asking for tickets.
Girl: Oh, I've sold mine. I put a poster up at my football club and someone there wanted it.
Boy: That's good.
Girl: Yes, Dad put an advertisement online first, but no one called us about that.

🔊 10 Unit 5, Grammar, Exercise 3

Man: Last summer, Simon went camping with his family near a castle in the mountains in Scotland. It was a beautiful place, but as soon as they arrived, it started to rain and it didn't stop for days! During the day, they didn't do any activities because it was too wet outside, and at night, they didn't sleep because the wind and the rain were so noisy. After four days of rain, the man who lived in the castle invited them to stay with him at the castle! After that, Simon and his family had a great time. They didn't mind the bad weather because they played games in the castle all day and they didn't hear the rain and the wind at night.

🔊 11 Unit 5, Listening Part 2

Woman: The Branton Museum of Pop Music is the city's most popular museum for visitors aged 12 to 18. Its new location in Victoria Square is much more central than its old Green Street address.
This month, it has a new exhibition called 'Scoresound', that's spelled S-C-O-R-E-S-O-U-N-D, and it explores film music, with hundreds of pictures, recordings and videos. It's open from the 31st of October until the 25th of November.
The museum's also just opened a new fashion room. Here, you can see the clothes worn by some of the most famous pop stars of the last 50 years.
You can travel to the museum by car or bus, and you get a free poster with your entrance ticket.
Museum tickets for adults cost eight pounds fifty, but for schoolchildren up to the age of 19 it's just five pounds seventy-five. However, children under five go free.

◁) 12 Unit 6, Grammar, Exercise 4

1
Man: Journey A is shorter than journey B.
2
Man: Journey C is the shortest.
3
Man: Journey A is further than journey C.
4
Man: Journey B is the longest.
5
Man: Journey A is cheaper than journey B.
6
Man: Journey B is the most expensive.
7
Man: Train B is older than train C.
8
Man: Train C is the newest.

◁) 13 Unit 6, Vocabulary, Exercise 3

1
Boy: How do you usually travel when you go on holiday?
Girl: We usually travel by train.
2
Boy: Do most students walk to your school or do they go by bus or car?
Girl: Most go by car!
3
Boy: Which airport do people in your town fly from?
Girl: They usually fly from Manchester airport.
4
Boy: Can 10-year-olds drive cars in your country?
Girl: No, of course they can't!
5
Boy: Does anyone in your family ride a motorbike?
Girl: Yes. My uncle rides one.
6
Boy: How long does it take for a ship to sail around the world?
Girl: I don't know. How long?
Boy: About three months, I think.

◁) 14 Unit 6, Listening Part 5

Marcia: I'm going to start taking the school bus next week, Josh. Where should I catch it?
Josh: Well, I catch it from Hill Street. After the railway bridge, there's a roundabout, and my bus stop's there.
Marcia: OK. Does Max catch it there? He lives near you.
Josh: No. His mum drives him into town because she works at the motorbike shop. She leaves her car in the car park in George Street. Max catches the bus there.
Marcia: OK.
Josh: Oliver gets on at the bus stop in New Street, by the bridge – not the one near the cinema, the other one.
Marcia: Oh yes, I can catch it there, too. Who else goes on the bus?
Josh: Emily. She lives opposite the cinema, so she catches the bus there, not far from the tram stop.
Marcia: What about Katy, Emily's neighbour?
Josh: She doesn't like crossing the busy road, so she gets on the school bus next to the traffic lights behind the station.
Marcia: Oh yes.
Josh: Tom gets the bus too, at the crossing, near the supermarket.
Marcia: I know. Thanks, Josh.

◁) 15 Unit 7, Grammar, Exercise 4

Girl: Jack is always hungry in the afternoon at school.
Boy: He should eat more at lunchtime.
Girl: Jack often forgets what his homework is.
Boy: He should write it down in a diary or notebook.
Girl: When it rains, Jack's clothes always get wet.
Boy: He should take an umbrella.
Girl: Jack wants to play tennis better.
Boy: He should take some lessons.
Girl: Jack is always tired in the morning.
Boy: He shouldn't go to bed late.
Girl: Jack's sister is angry with him.
Boy: He shouldn't borrow her things without asking.

◁) 16 Unit 7, Vocabulary, Exercise 3

1
Boy: Hassan only has lessons at school in the morning.
2
Boy: Hassan studies 14 different subjects at school.
3
Boy: A man called Mr Ali teaches Hassan maths.
4
Boy: Hassan spends about two hours a night doing his homework.
5
Boy: Hassan only missed one day of school this year.
6
Boy: Hassan was very happy when he passed his exams last year.

◁) 17 Unit 7, Listening Part 2

Woman: I'm here to tell you about my after-school music lessons here at Hilltop school. I'm Mrs Clarke. I know some of you can already play the violin because you learn it in music lessons at school. But if you'd like to try something else, you can learn to play the guitar with me. I have a class of ten students, and we have lots of fun! You have school band practice on Mondays, and then a free afternoon on Tuesdays. My lessons are on Wednesdays, starting at four o'clock and finishing at five thirty. We meet in the big room opposite Art Room 7 – it's Room 58. If you come, you must buy the book I use so you can practise at home. It's called *Improve* and you can buy it at Records, the music shop in the town centre. My lessons aren't expensive, because you learn in a group of ten. Each student pays just £23.20 a month, so it's about £5.80 a week. OK? Any questions?

◁) 18 Unit 8, Grammar, Exercise 3

1
Man: He didn't stop laughing while he was watching the cartoon.
2
Man: The bowl fell on her foot while she was putting fruit in it.
3
Man: They saw the circus lorries in the street while they were walking to school.
4
Man: He broke the light on his bike while he was trying to repair the wheel.
5
Man: She was playing a computer game, so she didn't hear the phone.
6
Man: We built a fire for the first time while we were camping.

🔊 19 Unit 8, Listening Part 5

Matthew: How was your holiday, Alice?
Alice: Great, thanks, Matthew. My course was really interesting.
Matthew: What did you learn?
Alice: How to write stories and news articles.
Matthew: Really? That sounds interesting.
Alice: Ahmet did a course, too. He learned how to prepare Chinese dishes on holiday – he wants to work as a food writer when he leaves school.
Matthew: Zena went to the same holiday camp, didn't she?
Alice: Yes, but she didn't need to do lots of reading and writing for her course. She had a week of Spanish dancing lessons.
Matthew: What about Zena's sister, Leah?
Alice: She learned to work with silver and made a beautiful necklace and earrings. I saw them yesterday.
Matthew: That's amazing! Is Mick still on holiday?
Alice: No, he had to come home on Monday to do a music exam. But before that, he did a windsurfing and sailing course at Lake Jarvis.
Matthew: Cool! When does Ellie come home?
Alice: Next week. She's doing a short course on biology this week. It's all about water plants and she loves it.
Matthew: Really?

🔊 20 Unit 9, Grammar, Exercise 2

1
Man: She's putting her violin in its case because she's going to have a music lesson.
2
Man: He's studying hard because he's going to do an exam tomorrow.
3
Man: He's phoning his mum from school because he isn't going to go home for dinner.
4
Man: He's finding his seat in the theatre because the play is going to start soon.
5
Man: He's waiting in the street because a bus is going to come soon.
6
Man: She's putting her sweater in her bag because it is going to be cold this evening.
7
Man: He isn't enjoying the football match because his team isn't going to win.

🔊 21 Unit 9, Listening Part 4

1 *You will hear a girl talking about a job she wants to do. What does she want to be?*
Girl: At school, I enjoy my art lessons, especially photography. My art teacher gave me some tips about taking great pictures on a trip to Kripps Lake. I also enjoy writing stories and finding out about people's lives. So I'd really like to put all those things together, and get a job on a newspaper or a magazine. But I don't think that'll be easy!
2 *You will hear Ravi talking to his dad. What are they discussing?*
Male: Haven't you got to do some maths exercises before dinner, Ravi? It's going to be ready in an hour.
Boy: I'll do them later, Dad – I want to watch a basketball game.

Male: You must do them before you watch TV.
Boy: OK. I'll do them now. I'll watch the game online after dinner.
Male: Fine.
3 *You will hear Holly talking about going to the library. Why is she going there?*
Girl: After my last lesson, I'm going to the school library. I need a book for my history research and they don't have it on the shelves – I checked online today. So I'm going to ask Mrs Stewart at the library to get it for me. She's really nice. I did this before, and the book arrived in about three days. I took it back yesterday.
4 *You will hear Rosie telling her mum about an exhibition. What was wrong with the exhibition?*
Woman: So why didn't you enjoy the exhibition, Rosie?
Girl: Well, Mum, there were lots of interesting paintings. I just wasn't sure what most of them were, or what they meant.
Woman: Oh. There are usually signs next to the pictures which tell you about them.
Girl: Not for this exhibition. There was just one poster, about the painter's life.
Woman: That's a pity.
5 *You will hear a boy talking to his mum about lunch. What is he going to make for lunch?*
Boy: I'm going to make lunch for us, Mum. There are lots of vegetables in the fridge – I'll cut them into little pieces and heat them in a pan with some water and some tomatoes, and lots of pepper and salt… and perhaps a bit of pasta. Then we'll have a nice hot bowl of it with some bread. OK?
Girl: Sounds lovely!

🔊 22 Unit 10, Grammar, Exercise 3

1
Man: She'll go to the lake with Nick if he doesn't have football practice.
2
Man: If she goes to the lake, she'll need her swimming costume.
3
Man: If she takes a picnic, she won't need to buy food in the café.
4
Man: If she cycles around the lake, she'll feel tired.
5
Man: If she sees some interesting animals, she'll take photos of them.
6
Man She'll put her camera in her bag if it starts to rain.
7
Man: She won't take her umbrella if the weather's good.

🔊 23 Unit 10, Listening Part 1

1 *What was the weather like last winter?*
Boy: Look at the snow outside, Daisy!
Daisy: Wow! We can go skiing this weekend – brilliant! We didn't ski last winter at all, did we?
Boy: No, it was too wet. But there may be a lot of ice on the roads this weekend, so we may not go skiing.
Daisy: Never mind.
2 *Who will go for the birthday meal with Jade and her parents?*
Mum: Who's coming to the restaurant with us on your birthday, Jade?
Jade: I asked three of my best friends, Mary, Kate and Emma, but Emma can't come.
Mum: OK … and of course your brother will be with us.
Jade: Yes, and you and dad.
Mum: Of course! We're looking forward to it!

3 *What happened during the storm last week?*

Boy: That storm was terrible last week, wasn't it?

Girl: Yes! A tree fell across the river and the water came up onto the road near our school.

Boy: Was the school OK?

Girl: Yes, but we had to walk there every morning until the water went away. Cars couldn't get to the school, but it was OK on foot.

4 *What does Eleanor do on the farm at weekends?*

Eleanor: I usually go to my uncle's farm at weekends.

Man: Really? Where's the farm, Eleanor?

Eleanor: It's the one next to the horse-riding school.

Man: Cool! And you told me that he has lots of chickens – do you collect their eggs?

Eleanor: I do, and my friend Sue sells them in the farm shop. It's really good fun.

5 *Where is Charlie's phone?*

Girl: Why are you using my phone, Charlie?

Charlie: Because mine's in Mum's car and she's gone to see Grandma.

Girl: Are you sure? I saw it in the kitchen this morning.

Charlie: I know, but I went to the library after that. Mum drove me home, and she's just texted Dad to say she found it on one of the seats.

🔊 24 Unit 11, Grammar, Exercise 3

Dad: Hi, Adam. What are you doing? Have you had dinner yet?

Adam: No, I've just got home from my music lesson.

Dad: Oh, are you hungry?

Adam: Yes, I am. Do you want me to help you cook?

Dad: No, I've already done it. I made some fish soup earlier this evening, so it's all ready.

Adam: Great! Let's eat. I'll lay the table.

Dad: I've already done that too. But I haven't put any water or glasses on the table yet. Can you do that, please?

Adam: OK.

🔊 25 Unit 11, Listening Part 3

Christina: Hello, Leo.

Leo: What's the matter, Christina?

Christina: I've hurt my back.

Leo: Oh no! Have you seen the doctor?

Christina: Not yet. But I'm going to.

Leo: This morning?

Christina: No, I couldn't get an appointment – I'm going tomorrow afternoon. So I won't be at school until Thursday.

Leo: How did you do it?

Christina: Well, I walked home after basketball practice yesterday, and then it happened when I was going upstairs to the flat.

Leo: Really? So where are you now?

Christina: At home, lying down. Not on my bed, in the living room, on the sofa. Mum's here, making lunch in the kitchen.

Leo: So what activities can you do? You can't come skateboarding this evening, can you?

Christina: Mum says no, which I'm not pleased about. But swimming's OK – it may help. I'm not having my guitar lesson this evening, but that's fine!

Leo: Would you like something to read? I've got some good books about famous people.

Christina: OK – but I don't want to read about film actors. Maybe something about a pop star?

Leo: I've got nothing like that. There's one about a footballer – what about that?

Christina: Brilliant. Thanks, Leo.

🔊 26 Unit 12, Grammar, Exercise 3

1

Man: The first email was sent in 1971.

2

Man: The first digital cameras were sold by a company called Logitech.

3

Man: The first fridge was built by Jacob Perkins in 1834.

4

Man: The first computer mouse was made of wood.

5

Man: The first hairdryer was used by a French hairdresser.

6

Man: The first text messages were written on the third of December, 1992.

🔊 27 Unit 12, Listening Part 5

Woman: It's very quiet, Alice.

Girl: I know, Mum! Everyone's looking for something on the internet.

Woman: Even Dad?

Girl: Yes, he wants to download a movie – that one about the piano player.

Woman: Your brother wants to see that. What's *he* looking for?

Girl: He's looking for an electric guitar – he wants to start learning before our holiday.

Woman: I'll ask your sister to help him. What's she trying to find?

Girl: She's looking for a printer that'll work with her new tablet. ... You know our cousin's here?

Woman: Really?

Girl: She was looking for a better tablet, but couldn't find one she wanted. Now she's searching for a digital camera to take on holiday.

Woman: Aunt Jane will be pleased.

Girl: Yes, she phoned earlier. She's looking on the internet because she wants a tablet that she saw on TV. That's for their holiday, too, so she can download pictures from her camera.

Woman: Can't you take pictures with a tablet? By the way, you know Grandma's going with them?

Girl: Yes. She says she needs a clock to travel with, so she's looking at a website now, then she's going to watch TV.

Woman: Right!

Acknowledgements

Author Acknowledgements

Frances Treloar would like to thank Helena and Pete for their support.

Publishers acknowledgements

The authors and publishers are grateful and would like to extend a special thanks to Sarah Dev-Sherman (Project Manager), Sheila Thorne (Editor), Leon Chambers (Audio Producer), Soundhouse Studios, and Wild Apple Design.

In addition, the publishers and authors would like to thank the following for their role in reviewing the material in general and in particular those who participated in the development of the exam tasks: Jane Coates, Sara Georgina Vargas Ochoa, Cressida Hicks, Annie Broadhead, Anthony Cosgrove, Sarah Dymond, Joanna Kosta, Darren Longley, Sheila Thorne, Catriona Watson-Brown.

Development of this publication has made use of the Cambridge English Corpus (CEC). The CEC is a computer database of contemporary spoken and written English, which currently stands at over one billion words. It includes British English, American English and other varieties of English. It also includes the Cambridge Learner Corpus, developed in collaboration with the University of Cambridge ESOL examinations. Cambridge University Press has built up the CEC in order to provide evidence of authentic language use to better inform the production of learning materials.

This product is also informed by English Profile, a collaborative programme designed to enhance the learning, teaching and assessment of English worldwide. Its main partners are Cambridge University Press and Cambridge ESOL exams and its aim is create a profile for English usage based on the Common European Framework of Reference for Languages (CEFR). English Profile outcomes, such as the English Vocabulary Profile provide detailed information based on language level and help inform the language that learners can be expected to demonstrate at each CEFR level, offering a clear benchmark for learner's proficiency. For more information, please visit www.englishprofile.org.

The authors and publishers acknowledge the following sources of copyright material and are grateful for the permissions granted. While every effort has been made, it has not always been possible to identify the sources of all the material used, or to trace all copyright holders. If any omissions are brought to our notice, we will be happy to include the appropriate acknowledgements on reprinting and in the next update to the digital edition, as applicable.

Key: U = Unit, Vocab = Vocabulary

Photography

The following images are sourced from Getty Images.

U1: Nicolas Russell/The Image Bank; Neustockimages/iStock/Getty Images Plus; Kemter/E+; Juanmonino/iStock/Getty Images Plus; Joan Vicent Cantó Roig/E+; Juanmonino/E+; SensorSpot/E+; SolStock/E+; Alys Tomlinson/DigitalVision; Fgorgun/iStock/Getty Images Plus; Hero Images; **U2**: WIN-Initiative/Neleman/Riser; Stefanie Aumiller/Cultura; John Fedele/Blend Images; Dmitry Naumov/Moment; Andrea De La Parra Valdes/EyeEm; AlenPopov/E+; Juanmonino/E+; Patrik Giardino/Photodisc; Echo/Juice Images; Guido Mieth/Moment; Caiaimage/Robert Daly; **U3**: Dorling Kindersley; trigga/iStock/Getty Images Plus; Diamond Sky Images/DigitalVision; milanfoto/E+; Rosemary Calvert/Photographer's Choice; Vesna Jovanovic/EyeEm; Tim Hawley/Photolibrary; Tastyart Ltd Rob White/Photolibrary; Daly and Newton/OJO Images; Absodels; xavierarnau/E+; Caiaimage/Paul Bradbury; **U4**: Maskot; Jena Ardell/Moment; **U5**: Jay's photo/Moment; Red Chopsticks; Johner Images; Rob Lewine; DigiPub/Moment; Museimage/Moment; Blend Images - Erik Isakson/Brand X Pictures; **U6**: Hristo Rusev/NurPhoto; Hero Images; WIN-Initiative/Neleman; 5m3photos/Moment; ColorBlind Images/Blend Images; Brian Hagiwara/Photolibrary; Design Pics/Bilderbuch; **U7**: Sawitree Pamee/EyeEm; Blend Images - KidStock/Brand X Pictures; KidStock/Blend Images; Sorin Rechitan/EyeEm; **U8**: Hero Images; svetikd/E+; Shestock/Blend Images; PeopleImages/E+; View Pictures/Universal Images Group; Andrew Brookes/Cultura; **U9**: Kevin Mazur/Getty Images Entertainment; Gary Gershoff/WireImage; Paul Zimmerman/WireImage; Hill Street Studios/Blend Images; kali9/E+; Rolf Bruderer/Blend Images; Hero Images; **U10**: cenkerdem/DigitalVision Vectors; **U11**: SensorSpot/E+; JGI/Jamie Grill/Blend Images; steele2123/E+; Juanmonino/E+; Photodisc; Letizia Le Fur/ONOKY; Paul Burns; Sitthiphong Thadakun/EyeEm; Henn Photography/Cultura; **U12**: ralphgillen/iStock Editorial/Getty Images Plus; Alessandro De Carli/EyeEm; Creative Crop/DigitalVision; Nastco/iStock/Getty Images Plus; Jeffrey Coolidge/DigitalVision; Tolga Tezcan/E+; Nerthuz/iStock/Getty Images Plus; grebeshkovmaxim/iStock/Getty Images Plus; RadeLukovic/iStock/Getty Images Plus; Cginspiration/E+; Ron Levine/DigitalVision; Bloom Productions/Taxi; Juanmonino/iStock/Getty Images Plus; **Vocab**: skynesher/E+; Anetlanda/iStock/Getty Images Plus; fatihhoca/E+; Frederic Cirou/PhotoAlto Agency RF Collections; Andreas Stamm; Andreas Ulvdell/Folio; Ems-Forster-Productions/DigitalVision; Westend61; Morsa Images/DigitalVision; RunPhoto/Photodisc; Suriyapong Koktong/EyeEm; bjeayes/iStock/Getty Images Plus; Jena Ardell/Moment; Carolyn Plummer/EyeEm; Niels Busch/Cultura; Hendrik Sulaiman/EyeEm; Roman Samokhin/iStock/Getty Images Plus; Jiang Jiahao/EyeEm; Marc Casas Borras/EyeEm; Gail Shotlander/Moment; Ramzi Rizk/EyeEm; Chris Jongkind/Moment; Martin Konopka/EyeEm; Kira Eisenach/EyeEm; Branislav Novak/EyeEm; Pete Ark/Moment; Sir Francis Canker Photography/Moment; Stewart Hardy/Moment; kumacore/Moment; Photographer Renzi Tommaso/Moment; Chris Hepburn/Photodisc; targovcom/iStock/Getty Images Plus.

The below image has been sourced from other source.
U8: Courtesy of Tree hotel.

Front cover photography by William King/The Image Bank/Getty Images; Sir Francis Canker Photography/Moment/Getty Images; vladj55/iStock/Getty Images Plus/Getty Images; fitopardo.com/Moment/Getty Images; EnginKorkmaz/iStock Editorial/Getty Images Plus/Getty Images; Hero Images/Getty Images.

Illustration

Jo and Alina from KJA Agency; Giuliano Aloisi from Advocate Art.

Audio

Audio recordings by Leon Chambers. Recorded at The Soundhouse Studios, London.